ESTATE PLANNING
workbook

ESTATE PLANNING
workbook

A Companion to
You Can't Take It
With You

S A N D R A   E .   F O S T E R

John Wiley & Sons Canada Limited
22 Worcester Road
Etobicoke, Ontario
M9W 1L1

The National Library of Canada Cataloguing in Publication Data:

Foster, Sandra E., 1955-
    Estate planning workbook : a companion to you can't take it
with you

ISBN 0-470-83177-4

    1. Estate planning--Canada--Popular works. I. Title.

KE5974.Z82F67 2001 Suppl.   332.024'01   C2001-903617-5

Production Credits
Cover & interior text design: Interrobang Graphic Design Inc.
Printer: Tri-Graphic Printing Ltd.

Printed in Canada
10 9 8 7 6 5 4 3 2 1

Contents

Preface

I've been asked many times to offer an expanded version of the checklists, worksheets, and personal inventory forms that were originally published in *You Can't Take It With You: The Common-Sense Guide to Estate Planning for Canadians*. In response to these requests, I have developed this workbook as a companion to *You Can't Take It With You*.

This workbook will help you work through, on a personal level, the concepts that are discussed in *You Can't Take It With You* and consider much of what you need to think about as you develop your personal estate plan. While there are brief explanations throughout this workbook, this workbook does not contain all the information related to the strategies and tips you'll find in *You Can't Take It With You*. Rather, it's best used as a companion book to help you consider how the concepts of estate planning might apply to your personal situation.

Perhaps you, like many Canadians, have not yet taken the time to prepare an estate plan or to update your existing estate plan. But if you have named a beneficiary on your RRSP, RRIF, life insurance, or employee benefits, you have already made financial decisions that affect your financial and estate plan. Even the way you register the title of your home or your investment accounts can affect your estate plan.

Some people find just thinking about what they want to happen, should they become incapacitated or die, very stressful. Others don't know what their choices are or who to name in their estate planning documents, so their estate plan takes a backseat to the activities of day-to-day life. Remember, you don't do estate planning for yourself—you do it for those you leave behind.

The information in this workbook can help you:

- take a snapshot of your current financial situation

- determine your estate planning objectives

- better understand some of the wording used in legal documents

- estimate the current value of your estate

- make it easier for the person named in your power of attorney, representative agreement, or mandate documents to follow your instructions and locate all the information they need to make decisions on your behalf in the event you become mentally incapacitated

- make it easier for your executor to locate all your personal and financial documents to carry out the instructions in your will and wrap up your estate

- identify key questions for your lawyer, financial advisor, accountant, or other professional

While there can be a lot to consider related to your estate plan, it is not necessary to complete all the information in this workbook in one sitting or to make all the decisions on your own. I recommend you work through it a bit at a time—focusing only on those areas that apply to your personal situation. Throughout the workbook, you'll find space where you can make notes or write down questions related to your own situation to discuss with your own advisors.

Let's get practical!

WORDS OF CAUTION

Family law and the laws related to wills, powers of attorney, trusts, living wills, and probate fees vary from province to province. While the intention may be similar, each province has its own legislation, and lawyers include clauses in their documents that are appropriate for where you live.

This book discusses general issues to consider in preparing an estate plan. It is not intended to be a do-it-yourself estate plan. It is not a legal document or a tax guide and does not provide legal advice. There is no guarantee that this workbook covers every possible situation or scenario. The author, publisher, and distributor are not liable for any claims, losses, or damages of any kind arising out of the use of this book.

This workbook is offered for educational purposes only. It does not provide any legal, tax, or financial advice, and the author and publisher make no representations or warranties about the information in this book. The information in this book is of a general nature to help you understand the language of estate planning and some of the choices available to you.

It is sold with the understanding that the information that follows is not a substitute for consulting a professional who can apply the most current tax, trust, estate, succession, and family laws of your province to your particular situation. If you are an American, married to an American, hold a green card, or your children are American, you should consult a professional who is familiar with the U.S. estate planning issues.

The analysis in this book represents the opinion of the author and the legislation in effect at the time of publication, as well as changes that have been announced by the government that may not have been formally passed into law. Care has been taken to ensure the accuracy of the information contained in this book at the time it was published.

Readers are encouraged to obtain professional legal, tax, and financial advice on how these ideas might fit their own situation before deciding on a course of action.

CHAPTER ONE

Introduction

"Some people's money is merited
And other people's is inherited."
—*Ogden Nash*

Estate planning. Just the words are enough to intimidate many Canadians. After all, almost half of all Canadians adults have never taken the time to prepare a will. But your estate plan doesn't have to be complicated. Part of your estate plan can be very simple—making sure your paperwork and financial details are organized so your executor or representative can pull together your financial life on your behalf.

If you do not take the time to prepare your own estate plan, the government has rules it must follow to protect your assets in the event you become incapacitated, and intestacy rules to determine who gets what in the event you die without a will.

But estate planning involves more than determining what you want done with your assets on your death and writing a will. It should also include who would have the authority to make decisions for you in the event an accident or illness leaves you unable to make your own financial or personal decisions.

One simple definition of estate planning refers to those assets that are distributed according to the instructions in your will. But today, many people have structured their estate so that some of their assets are distributed outside the will, by naming a beneficiary (for their RRSP, RRIF, or life insurance), or by owning assets jointly (such as a joint bank account). Your estate plan really should consider *all* your assets and the different ways they can be distributed, not just the assets that will flow into your estate to be distributed according to your will.

A proper estate plan will consider your overall estate to help ensure that your beneficiaries will benefit the way you want and that your estate is distributed as quickly as possible. It can help make sure you pay no more in taxes or other fees than is absolutely necessary. A sound estate plan requires taking stock of your current financial situation, assessing your priorities, designing your estate plan, documenting your plan, and periodically reviewing that plan. This workbook is intended to help you work through many of these considerations, and in the process, to get organized.

While I have had all my estate planning documents in place and all my financial papers in one place (more or less) for quite some time, I also realized that my executor or attorney would not automatically understand my filing system. So I've completed my worksheets to help my representatives sort through everything. This workbook can help you to be clear and organize your financial documents and papers too.

HOW TO GET THE MOST FROM THIS WORKBOOK

To get the most from this estate planning workbook, I recommend you go through the information in this workbook in the order that makes the most sense for your situation. You don't have to start at the beginning and work your way through it to the end. Don't try to complete all the information in one sitting.

The information in this workbook can also help you prepare for meetings with your estate planning professionals and maybe even reduce the time you spend with them. And we all know that "time is money."

When completing these worksheets, don't guess at the details. The more accurate your information, the more helpful it will be, when the time comes.

Once your workbook is complete, keeping the information up to date will not take nearly as long. Annual updating seems to work well for most people, such as around tax time or near the end of the year.

Let's get started.

THE SIX Ds OF ESTATE PLANNING

There are six Ds of estate planning to putting together your estate plan:

- Decide
- Design
- Develop
- Discuss
- Document
- Distribute

The pages that follow will help you work on the six Ds of estate planning. If you already have an estate plan in place, remember that nothing stays the same, and you can use this workbook to review your current estate plan.

A FRAMEWORK FOR YOUR ESTATE PLAN

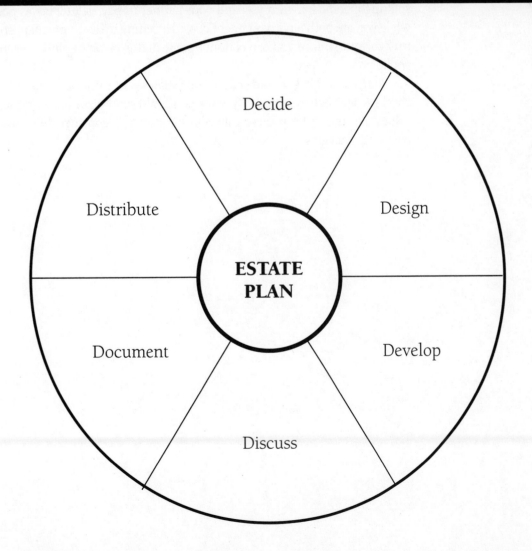

Decide

The beauty of making an estate plan is that you get to decide who gets what, how much they get, as well as when they get it. You can decide whether or not you want to leave as large an estate as possible, or whether you'd prefer to spend as much as you can before you go. (If you don't spend it, someone else probably will!)

You decide who you want to benefit from your assets when you are no longer here. While you cannot legally write anyone out of your will who is financially dependent on you, or in most provinces, leave your spouse less than he or she might have been entitled to had you divorced, your estate plan truly is your statement of your wishes.

Your estate plan should also reflect the needs of your beneficiaries. For example, if you have beneficiaries who will be underage, you will need to set up a trust in your will to have the assets managed until they are older—unless you want the public trustee of your province to do this. If you have beneficiaries who will never be any good at managing money, you might want to consider how much they should receive outright. If you have been diligent about splitting income between you and your partner to pay as little tax as possible while you are both alive, you might consider setting up a testamentary spousal trust in your will, so you can continue some of this income splitting even after you're gone.

Your estate plan should reflect your values and priorities. The following checklist will help you identify your personal estate planning priorities and values. Be sure to keep these values in mind as you consider different estate planning strategies.

YOUR ESTATE PLANNING PRIORITIES CHECKLIST

This checklist is designed to help you with the "Decide" step of estate planning. It will help you identify your estate planning priorities. As you work through the rest of this workbook, you can refer to this checklist to help you ensure your estate plan reflects your long-term goals and objectives.

I agree/disagree with the following statements:

	Strongly Agree	Agree	Neither Agree or Disagree	Disagree	Strongly Disagree	Not Applicable
I want to enjoy my money while I am alive.	❑	❑	❑	❑	❑	❑
I want to leave everything to my spouse or partner.	❑	❑	❑	❑	❑	❑
I want to treat my common-law partner as if we were married.	❑	❑	❑	❑	❑	❑
I would like my spouse or partner to enjoy the same standard of living after my death.	❑	❑	❑	❑	❑	❑
I want to indicate my choice of guardian to look after my children in the event my spouse and I die before they reach the age of majority.	❑	❑	❑	❑	❑	❑
I want my children to benefit equally from my estate.	❑	❑	❑	❑	❑	❑
I have children from a previous marriage and I want to keep an inheritance for them separate in my plans.	❑	❑	❑	❑	❑	❑
I would like to be able to pay for my children and grandchildren's post-secondary education.	❑	❑	❑	❑	❑	❑
I don't want my children/grandchildren to receive their inheritance too early.	❑	❑	❑	❑	❑	❑
I want to minimize the final tax bill sent to Canada Customs and Revenue Agency.	❑	❑	❑	❑	❑	❑
I want to minimize the final tax bill sent to another tax jurisdiction, such as the U.S. Internal Revenue Service.	❑	❑	❑	❑	❑	❑
I want to minimize all costs and fees required to settle my estate.	❑	❑	❑	❑	❑	❑
I want make a significant donation to charity after my death.	❑	❑	❑	❑	❑	❑

	Strongly Agree	Agree	Neither Agree or Disagree	Disagree	Strongly Disagree	Not Applicable
I want to be remembered with a simple funeral or memorial service.	❏	❏	❏	❏	❏	❏
I don't want to transfer any assets to my beneficiaries until I'm sure I no longer require them for my own needs, that is after my death.	❏	❏	❏	❏	❏	❏
I want to maximize the value of my estate so I can leave as much as possible to my beneficiaries.	❏	❏	❏	❏	❏	❏
I believe that an inheritance is a gift and that my beneficiaries should consider whatever they might get as a bonus.	❏	❏	❏	❏	❏	❏
I want to ensure that my debts will be paid off on my death.	❏	❏	❏	❏	❏	❏
I am concerned that I might not have the right amount of life insurance.	❏	❏	❏	❏	❏	❏
I want to put a succession plan in place to ensure the family business can stay in the family.	❏	❏	❏	❏	❏	❏
I want to keep the vacation property in the family.	❏	❏	❏	❏	❏	❏
I want to integrate my estate plan with my retirement and tax plan.	❏	❏	❏	❏	❏	❏
I want my organs or tissues to be donated when I no longer require them.	❏	❏	❏	❏	❏	❏
I want to choose who will make decisions on my behalf, should I become incapacitated.	❏	❏	❏	❏	❏	❏
I want to ensure that my will and other estate planning cannot be challenged.	❏	❏	❏	❏	❏	❏
I want to organize my financial affairs so my power of attorney and executor can act on my behalf, with the minimal amount of stress.	❏	❏	❏	❏	❏	❏
Other _____	❏	❏	❏	❏	❏	❏
Other _____	❏	❏	❏	❏	❏	❏

Design and Develop

There are many ways you can set up your estate plan to achieve your estate planning objectives. There are ways to reduce the cost of dying; there are tax-effective ways to leave an inheritance to a beneficiary. There are many ways to register your assets, and even to distribute your assets.

The estate plan you design and develop will be unique to your personal and financial situation.

For more information on the many options and tools that are available to you to design and develop an estate plan that will achieve your goals, I invite you to read *You Can't Take It With You: The Common-Sense Guide to Estate Planning*.

Document

Let's be realistic. How easy would it be for someone to quickly pull together the personal and financial details of your life?

Many people, even if they haven't taken the time to prepare an estate plan, have statements and paperwork all over the place (they may even have trouble finding the paperwork needed to complete their personal tax return each year). Imagine how difficult it could be for someone else to access all the relevant information that is needed, not just to do your final tax return, but to wrap up all the details of your life? In the event you become mentally incapacitated, your power of attorney or representative needs to locate all your personal and financial information to be able to make decisions on your behalf. On your death, your executor needs to locate all your personal and financial information, as well as locate your beneficiaries and anyone else you have named in your will.

You also need to properly document your estate plan to ensure it will be carried out. If you fail to have valid estate planning documents, the government has a "default" plan that must be followed and that may not settle your estate the way you want.

Naming beneficiaries on your RRSPs, RRIFs, life insurance, annuities, and company pension plans, as appropriate, is part of documenting your estate planning. If you need to revise your designated beneficiary, it's not enough just to e-mail your financial institution the new name or to tell them over the phone. You must put your request in writing. Your financial institution can provide you with the correct form to use. Complete it, sign it, and return it to them.

I've found that many Canadians are intimidated by the legal wording found in wills, power of attorney documents for finances and personal and health care. In Chapters 2 and 3, I've included sample clauses you might find in these documents to illustrate the wording that might be used. These documents should not be used to prepare your own estate planning documents.

The information in this workbook is not meant to imply that your estate planning documents are correct or incorrect. That is a question to ask your lawyer. I offer this information to help demystify some of this wording and help you better understand your estate planning choices, and what your lawyer or notary is talking about.

In Chapters 4, 5 and 6, you'll find worksheets where you can document all the information relevant to your personal and financial situation—the people in your life, your assets and liabilities, as well as the location of all your estate planning documents. These worksheets can help protect your assets and ensure nothing is missed. As you work through these worksheets, complete only the information that applies to your situation and ignore the rest.

The completed worksheets can also provide your partner and those close to you with the details they need to help them after your death. Many people find that their memory is affected while they are grieving—having the information written down could help them work through what needs to be done. In conjunction with your legal estate planning documents, completing the information in this workbook can provide those you leave behind with most of the information they need to be able to carry out your instructions.

Discuss

Be sure to discuss your plans with your family and those people who are close to you. You should also discuss your estate plan with anyone you have assigned a job on your estate plan, including your executor, power of attorney, mandate, representative, guardians for any minor children, and the trustees of any trusts you establish. These people are not mind readers and will not be able to guess what you want done or why you want some things handled a certain way. They may not even be aware of all their duties and responsibilities. In the appendices, you'll find lists of the general duties and responsibilities of the executor and the representative for financial decisions and for personal and health care decisions.

They do not have to know all the details of your estate plan, but they should know enough to tell you if they would be willing to act on your behalf when the time comes.

Remember, you will not have the opportunity to explain your decisions after your death and may not have the opportunity in the event you become incapacitated. Take the time while you would be able, to ensure those involved appreciate your decisions, even if they do not agree with you.

Distribute

Some people want to help out while they are alive and choose to distribute some of their estate as gifts to family members or friends, or make charitable donations. Other people prefer to distribute their assets after death, just to make sure they don't give away money or assets they might need. After death, they can be sure they won't need them any more.

It may take many weeks or over a year for the estate trustee to pay all your outstanding debts and final income taxes and distribute your estate to your beneficiaries according to the instructions in your will.

In addition to spending your own money and giving away assets while you are alive, there are six main ways to distribute your estate:

1. according to the intestate rules of your province if you die without a will. This is not recommended. Your estate would be distributed according to the "one size fits all" rules. This is the default option, not a plan.

2. by naming beneficiaries on life insurance policies, pension plans, RRSPs, and RRIFs

3. through joint ownership of property

4. through the wording in any trusts you set up, either while you are alive or in your will

5. according to the instructions in a partnership or shareholder agreement you may have for your business interests and/or

6. according to the instructions in your will

The strategies you use to distribute your estate will depend on your personal situation. Some estate plans are more complex than others, but many estate plans are not complex.

GIFTS WHILE YOU ARE ALIVE

Do you also want to make any gifts to family or friends while you are alive? The gift could be of cash, investments, property, or anything else of value.

Yes   *No*
❏   ❏

Name	Item	Value of Item or Gift	When?
_____	_____	_____	_____
_____	_____	_____	_____
_____	_____	_____	_____

Do you want to make any gifts to charity while you are alive?

Yes   *No*
❏   ❏

Name of Charity	Item	Value of Item or Gift	When?
_____	_____	_____	_____
_____	_____	_____	_____
_____	_____	_____	_____

THE ESTATE PLANNING CHECKLIST

The first step in developing or reviewing your estate plan is to look at your current situation, to know where you are today, and to assess what you want to do. An estate plan, like any plan, reflects your situation and what you want to do at the time it is prepared.

Take this quiz. Any *No* or *Unsure* answers may require special attention as you work through this workbook and consult with your professional advisors.

Yes	No	Unsure	
❏	❏	❏	Have you prepared and signed a will?
❏	❏	❏	Have you prepared documents in the event of mental incapacity?
❏	❏	❏	Have you prepared and signed a financial power of attorney?
❏	❏	❏	Have you recently reviewed your will and power of attorney?
❏	❏	❏	Are your will and power of attorney for financial matters up to date?
❏	❏	❏	If you are married or cohabitating, have you taken steps to protect any assets you brought into the relationship?
❏	❏	❏	Have you named beneficiaries and alternative beneficiaries for your RRSPs, annuities, life insurance policies, LIFs and RRIFs, pension plans, and/or DPSPs?
❏	❏	❏	Are your beneficiary designations up to date?
❏	❏	❏	Have you named a backup executor in your will and backup powers of attorney?
❏	❏	❏	Have you provided for all your dependents?
❏	❏	❏	Have you provided for your spouse so he or she will not have to make a claim against your estate under provincial family laws?
❏	❏	❏	Have you estimated your income tax due on death?
❏	❏	❏	Have you left assets to your spouse which can be rolled over tax-free?
❏	❏	❏	Have you estimated the cost to have your will probated after your death?
❏	❏	❏	Have you reviewed how best to register the ownership of assets?
❏	❏	❏	Do you have enough cash to pay the cost of dying—including income taxes and executor and probate fees—without forcing the sale of family assets?
❏	❏	❏	If you have specific wishes regarding your funeral, have you left instructions with your executor?
❏	❏	❏	Have you prepared a living will or medical directive?

Yes	No	Unsure	
❏	❏	❏	Have you prepared a power of attorney for personal care or a health care proxy?
❏	❏	❏	Have you documented your wishes regarding organ donations?
❏	❏	❏	Have you considered making a planned gift to charity?
❏	❏	❏	If you have a business, do you have a succession plan?
❏	❏	❏	Does your spouse/children/executor know the names and addresses of your professional advisors?
❏	❏	❏	Does your spouse/children/executor know where to find your financial records, income tax returns, bank accounts, safety deposit box, and insurance policies?
❏	❏	❏	Have you prepared a detailed record of all your assets and accounts?
❏	❏	❏	Have you prepared all the necessary documents (including will, living will, power of attorney) for your estate plan?
❏	❏	❏	Do you have all the information you need to complete your estate plan?
❏	❏	❏	Is your estate plan up-to-date?
❏	❏	❏	Are there ways to simplify your financial affairs so your estate can be settled more quickly?

Pre-Estate Planning Documents

Many people believe that all they need is a will to document their estate plan, to give their executor or personal representative the legal authority to make decisions on their behalf, after death. But who would manage your finances or give consent for necessary medical treatment on your behalf, if you were alive but for some reason could not make these decisions for yourself due to mental incompetency or incapacity due to infirmity? In one province, the legislation indicates that these documents can also apply to an individual who may not have been declared to be mentally incompetent, but where it has been proven to the courts that the person is, because of mental or physical infirmity arising from disease, age, or other cause, or by reason of habitual drunkenness or the use of drugs, unable to make their own decisions.

With properly executed pre-estate planning documents for finances and health and personal care, you can give the person(s) of your choice the legal authority to make decisions on your behalf should you become unable to make these decisions for yourself. These documents are referred to by a number of different names, including power of attorney documents, proxies, mandates, or representative agreements.

As with any personal representative, the person named should be someone you trust, who understands your personal values, and will follow your instructions or, if you have not left detailed instructions, will make decisions based on what he or she believes is in your best interest and will stand up for your wishes.

While you are not required to prepare these documents, the alternative, should you become unable to make your own decisions, is to have someone from the office of the provincial public guardian or trustee make these decisions, or to oversee the decisions made by your family.

I've seen many people who have wills, but are missing these key estate planning documents. Maybe this is because it is difficult to think you might ever be in a position where you could not make your own decisions. Yet it's a fact that Canadians are living longer. In the event you become incapacitated some day, I believe it is important to have someone of your own choosing to make these decisions on your behalf.

Although each province has different styles of pre-estate documents, the documents cover two main areas:

1. your financial affairs, in which you name person(s) to make financial decisions on your behalf, such as paying your bills, completing your tax returns, and making investment decisions

2. your personal and health care, in which you name person(s) to make decisions on your behalf related to lifestyle matters, such as where you will live, and health and medical matters, such as what medical treatment you will receive.

FOR FINANCIAL DECISIONS

What if you are seriously injured in an accident and lying in a coma? incapacitated by a stroke? dealing with a severely debilitating condition? These things happen, but as long as you are alive, decisions have to be made and your bills still have to be paid.

There's nothing that says you have to have a power of attorney document for property or financial affairs. The alternative, should you become mentally incapacitated and unable to make your own decisions, is to let an official from the office of the provincial public guardian or trustee look after your finances. Your immediate family or those close to you have no automatic right to manage your finances on your behalf—at least, not without obtaining court approval.

While some power of attorney documents may limit the attorney's powers to a specific transaction or period of time, such as closing the purchase of a new home while you are travelling, the document you prepare as part of your estate planning is one that you want to continue or endure in the event you become incapacitated.

This is a powerful document. It gives someone else the power to make any decision you could make (except decisions related to estate planning, such as prepare a will). Naming the wrong person to act as your attorney or representative could lead to major abuses of this power. While you can build some protections into the document, some people prefer to name someone they trust to make decisions on their behalf.

The person you appoint is referred to by different names, depending on the province you live in. This person may be called a representative, attorney, or your mandatary. See the following chart for the term used for your substitute decision-maker for finances in your province.

Who's Who for Property?

	Name of Representative	Name of Document
Alberta	attorney	Enduring Power of Attorney
British Columbia	representative	Representative Agreement for Property or Finances
Manitoba	attorney	Springing Power of Attorney
New Brunswick	attorney	Power of Attorney
Newfoundland	attorney	Enduring Power of Attorney
Nova Scotia	attorney	Enduring Power of Attorney
Ontario	attorney	Continuing Power of Attorney for Property
Prince Edward Island	attorney	Power of Attorney During Legal Incapacity
Quebec	mandatary	Mandate Given in Anticipation of Incapacity
Saskatchewan	attorney	Enduring Power of Attorney

You will find a list of the duties of a power of attorney or representative for financial decisions in Appendix B.

SAMPLE POWER OF ATTORNEY DOCUMENT FOR FINANCIAL DECISIONS

The sample clauses that appear in boxes in this section illustrate the wording you might find in an actual pre-estate document for financial decisions. The comments that follow provide a brief explanation of what each clause really means and some of their implications. The intention of the pre-estate document for financial affairs is similar across the country. The following example refers to terms used in Ontario.

---

1. Identification

This is a General Power of Attorney under the *Substitute Decisions Act*. This Power of Attorney is given by Thomas Ellis in the City of Toronto and the Province of Ontario.

This section identifies the individual giving the power of attorney for property by their full, proper name that can be matched to the name they use at their financial institutions. You must have attained the age of majority to prepare a power of attorney document for property or finances.

In each province, the document is recognized under specific provincial legislation. For example, in Ontario, it is the *Substitute Decisions Act*; in British Columbia, it is recognized under the B.C. *Representation Agreement Act*.

Unlike the power of attorney document you might sign at the bank that covers only the specific assets you hold there, a general power of attorney can cover all your financial assets.

---

2. Revocation

I revoke any prior Powers of Attorney for Property or Financial Affairs, or any Power of Attorney that affects my property given by me, except a Power of Attorney given at any bank or financial institution.

As long as you are mentally capable, you can revoke a power of attorney by informing anyone who may be operating under a previous power of attorney that it has been revoked.

You may have more than one power of attorney, such as your general enduring power of attorney and a separate power of attorney at your bank for your account(s) there. If you need to have more than one document, ensure that one does not revoke the other(s) and whether or not to name the same person, or different people, in these documents.

Your power of attorney can also be revoked by the Public Trustee or Public Curator (in Quebec) if your attorney is not acting in your best interest.

On death, your power of attorney for property is automatically revoked and the authority to manage your financial affairs is transferred to your executor.

This sample is provided for illustration only. Not to be copied.

3. Appointment

I appoint my wife, Terri Ellis, in the City of Toronto in the Province of Ontario, to be my Attorney in accordance with the *Powers of Attorney Act*.

The person named as your attorney or personal representative must be able to make good financial decisions on your behalf. He or she has to:

- act in your best interest (not their own) and in good faith
- avoid conflicts of interest
- exercise good judgement on your behalf
- maintain records
- consult with you wherever possible.

In other words, the person you select should be someone you trust unconditionally who also has the ability to do the job, and who agrees to be appointed.

If you appoint more than one person to act as your attorney, they are required to make decisions on your behalf together, unless you state they can act "jointly and severally," that is, they are authorized to make decisions together, or to act independently.

4. Substitution

In the event that my wife should be unable or unwilling to act or to continue to act as my Attorney, then I substitute and appoint my brother, David Ellis, in the City of Toronto and Province of Ontario, to be my Attorney for Property in accordance with the *Powers of Attorney Act* to do on my behalf anything that I can lawfully do by an Attorney.

It's a good idea to include the name of a substitute or backup attorney, who is willing and able to act on your behalf in the event the original cannot when the time comes.

If your first choice becomes unwilling or unable to act, or unable to continue to act, and you don't name an alternate or backup attorney, your power of attorney document could be revoked. Then the decision-maker of last resort—someone from the office of the provincial public guardian and trustee or someone appointed by the courts—would make or oversee the decisions made on your behalf.

5. Powers to Manage Property

I authorize my Attorney for Property to do on my behalf, anything that I can lawfully do by an attorney, and specifically anything in respect of property that I could do if capable of managing property, except make a Will, subject to the law and to any conditions or restrictions contained in this document, including make the following expenditures on my behalf:

a) those expenditures reasonably necessary for my support and care

b) those expenditures reasonably necessary for the support, education, and care of my dependents, and

c) those expenditures necessary to satisfy any other legal obligation I may have.

This sample is provided for illustration only. Not to be copied.

Unless restrictions are specified, a power of attorney document authorizes your "attorney" to act on your behalf for any financial act that you would legally be able to do, except prepare or change your will. They don't have to make exactly the same decisions you would make if you were able; they only have to make decisions that are in your best interest.

The powers you give might be general, giving them the power to take care of all your financial matters. Or the powers might be limited, such as to complete a specific transaction or for a specific period of time, such as selling a piece of real estate or, because you have difficulty getting out, acting on your behalf with the Income Security department regarding your Old Age Security cheques.

In addition to authorizing your attorney to pay for anything that is necessary for your own personal support and care, some lawyers recommend you specifically authorize your attorney to pay for anything necessary to provide for your dependents.

Some power of attorney documents for financial decisions spell out the specific powers being granted, as may be required under provincial legislation such as:

- sign all necessary documents
- collect debts
- manage or sell real estate
- mediate or arbitrate disputes
- hire professionals

You can provide additional guidance to the person(s) you appoint to act as your attorney by discussing your wishes with them. For example, suppose you were considering moving to a condo. If your attorney knows this, he or she might find it easier to sell your house, rather than trying to maintain it while you are in the hospital.

---

6. Power to Take Possession

I authorize my Attorney for Property to take physical possession of all my property, including any property held in a safety deposit box, property held in safekeeping by others on my behalf, and property held by others subject to some professional privilege, which privilege I waive for this purpose.

For greater certainty, my Attorney for Power shall be entitled to review my Will in order to be able to manage my estate in a manner that is sensitive thereto.

This clause gives your attorney the right to remove assets and to take possession of your investment and real property, if this enables him or her to better protect and manage your assets on your behalf.

If you want your decision-maker to make decisions that are both in your best interests and reflect the estate planning you have set up in your will, you can specify that your attorney can review your will to better understand your overall intentions.

This sample is provided for illustration only. Not to be copied.

7. Legal Representative

My Power of Attorney is my "legal representative" for the purpose of the *Income Tax Act*.

This clause provides your attorney with the authority to act as your representative when dealing with Canada Customs and Revenue Agency. Your attorney(s) can then request information related to previous tax returns, file your tax returns, and, if necessary, appeal your assessment.

8. Continuing and Enduring Power

In accordance with the *Powers Of Attorney Act*, I declare that this Power of Attorney may be exercised during any subsequent legal incapacity on my part. This indicates my intention that this document will be a continuing Power of Attorney for Property under the *Substitute Decisions Act, 1992*, and may be used during my incapacity to manage property.

This is a key clause in your pre-estate document for financial decisions. Without wording to this effect, the powers granted to the person named as your attorney could be revoked if you become mentally incompetent.

If you want your attorney to continue to have the authority to represent you, even if you become mentally incapable of making your own decisions, you have to state that you want the appointment to endure or continue to be effective.

9. Family Law Consent

If my spouse disposes of or encumbers any interest in a matrimonial home in which I have a right to possession under Part II of the *Family Law Act*, I authorize the Attorney named in this Power of Attorney for me and in my name to consent to the transaction as provided for in clause 21(1) (a) of the said Act.

The family or matrimonial home has special treatment in many provinces. No one, including your spouse, can sell or mortgage a matrimonial home without your written consent.

If you want your attorney to be able to sell or mortgage any property classified as a family or matrimonial home, you may need to state that you are giving your attorney the power to do so on your behalf under your province's family law legislation. For example, in Manitoba, your document would refer to the *Homestead Act*. In Ontario, it would refer to the *Family Law Act*.

10. Indemnification

The Attorney shall be fully and completely indemnified against all claims, actions and costs which may be incurred by or imposed on him or her in connection with the exercise of the said Powers of Attorney, as long as the Attorney was acting in good faith.

The indemnification clause provides your power of attorney with the assurance that, if they act in your best interest and in good faith, they do not have to worry that they would be sued by you in the future (should you regain capacity), your estate, or anyone else who may have relied on instructions from the attorney.

This sample is provided for illustration only. Not to be copied.

11. Reference to the *Provincial Mental Health Act*

In accordance with the *Powers of Attorney Act*, I declare that, after due consideration, I am satisfied that the authority conferred on the Attorney named in this Power of Attorney is adequate to provide for the competent and effectual management of my estate in case I should become a patient in a psychiatric facility and be certified as not competent to manage my estate under the *Mental Health Act*. I therefore direct that in that event, the Attorney named in this Power of Attorney may retain this Power of Attorney for the management of my estate by complying with section 56(2) of the *Mental Health Act* and in that case the Public Trustee shall not become committee of my estate as would otherwise be the case under the Act.

If preparing an enduring power of attorney in Ontario, the document should make reference to the *Mental Health Act*. In other provinces, the power of attorney would refer to the appropriate provincial legislation.

12. Declaration

I confirm that I am at least eighteen (18) years of age.

An individual may prepare a power of attorney for property for finances once they reach the age of majority, in some provinces they may be able to prepare a power of attorney for health care at a younger age.

13. Conditions and Restrictions

This Power of Attorney is subject to no conditions and restrictions.

Unless you include restrictions and conditions on what the attorney can do, the power of attorney document authorizes your attorney to act on your behalf for any financial act that you would legally be able to do (except prepare or change your will.)

Some people focus on selecting someone they can trust completely and place no conditions or restrictions on what they can do.

In some provinces, such as B.C., residents can, if they want, name a monitor who will monitor the actions of their named representative to determine whether or not they are performing their duties.

14. Compensation

My Attorney may take compensation out of my property for any work done by him, her, or them, in connection with this continuing power of attorney for property, in accordance with the prescribed fee scale established pursuant to sections 40(1) and 90 of the *Substitute Decisions Act* for the compensation of attorneys under a continuing Power of Attorney.

In some provinces, your attorney may be entitled to compensation according to a provincial fee scale, or other compensation you specify in your document.

The person acting as your attorney is also entitled to reimbursement for all reasonable expenses related to looking after your affairs, such as postage, and mileage to travel to your bank.

This sample is provided for illustration only. Not to be copied.

---

15. Effective Date

This continuing Power of Attorney for Property comes into effect as of the date it is signed and witnessed.

Some people prepare a power of attorney for financial decisions that is effective immediately; others prepare a document in which the attorney's powers are triggered by a certain event, such as when a physician certifies they have become mentally incapacitated.

16. Signing Formalities

I have signed this Continuing Power of Attorney for Property in the presence of both of the witnesses whose names appear below on this 21st day of January, 2002.

Thomas Ellis
_____
Thomas Ellis

We are the witnesses to this continuing Power of Attorney for Property. We have signed this Power of Attorney in the presence of the person whose name appears above, and in the presence of each other, on the date shown above. Neither one of us is the Attorney, a spouse or partner of the Attorney, a child of the grantor or person whom the granter has demonstrated a settled intention to treat as a child of the grantor, or is less than eighteen (18) years old. Neither one of us has any reason to believe that the grantor is incapable of giving a Power of Attorney for making decisions in respect of which instructions are contained in this Power of Attorney.

_____   _____
(signature of witness)   (signature of witness)

_____   _____
(address)   (address)

_____   _____
(occupation)   (occupation)

Power of attorney documents for financial decisions must be properly witnessed to reduce the potential for abuse, and all provinces appear to be moving to establish signing formalities that require two witnesses, similar to the signing formalities for a formal will. In Ontario, all power of attorney documents signed since 1995 require two witnesses who are not your spouse, child, or others who have certain close relationships with you. In some provinces, the person(s) named must also provide their written consent. In Quebec, your notary or lawyer will certify that you understood the contents and implications of the mandate document at the time it was prepared.

This sample is provided for illustration only. Not to be copied.

POWER OF ATTORNEY FOR FINANCES WORKSHEET

This worksheet is designed to help you think through some of the items you want included in your power of attorney for finances. This worksheet is *not* a legal document.

APPOINTMENT

Yes   *No*

❑   ❑   Do you want your spouse/partner to make financial decisions alone on your behalf?

If not, who would you like to make financial decisions on your behalf?

Name _____ Address _____

Name _____ Address _____

Name _____ Address _____

Yes   *No*

❑   ❑   Have you considered a professional trustee, such as a trust company?

Who would you like to act as your alternate, or backup attorney(s), if the above are unable or unwilling to do the job when the time comes?

Name _____ Address _____

Name _____ Address _____

Name _____ Address _____

Yes   *No*

❑   ❑   Have these people agreed to act as your attorney(s) or alternate?

If you are naming more than one person to act as your representative for finances, do you want them to make:

Yes   *No*

❑   ❑   all decisions together, i.e. jointly?

❑   ❑   decisions together, or separately?

POWERS YOU WANT YOUR POWER OF ATTORNEY TO HAVE

Do you want your decision-maker for financial matters to have the powers to:

Yes　*No*

❑　❑　take care of all your financial matters (except prepare or update your will), often referred to as general powers?

❑　❑　make decisions regarding your investment and RRSP/RRIF portfolios?

❑　❑　pay, out of your assets, for the costs related to your support and care?

❑　❑　pay, out of your assets, to support, educate, and care for your dependents?

❑　❑　give consent, on your behalf, regarding any property where you have rights under your province's family or matrimonial laws?

❑　❑　sign contracts and other legal documents on your behalf?

❑　❑　collect debts owed to you?

❑　❑　hire professionals to assist in the management of your property and fulfill your financial obligations?

❑　❑　manage and/or sell real estate?

❑　❑　manage and make decisions related to your business?

❑　❑　meditate or arbitrate disputes on your behalf?

❑　❑　review the instructions in your will to understand your long-term instructions?

❑　❑　be your legal representative with the Canada Customs and Revenue Agency?

❑　❑　other:_____

COMPENSATION

In addition to reimbursement for all reasonable out-of-pocket expenses related to looking after my financial affairs, I want my attorney for finances to receive:

❑　compensation that is equitable given the amount of time and expertise required to handle my financial affairs

❑　the sum of $ _____ annually

❑　compensation according to the provincial fee scale. In some provinces, this is nil.

❑　nothing

Yes　*No*

❑　❑　Have you discussed compensation with your attorney?

EFFECTIVE DATE

I would like this enduring document for financial decisions to become effective:

❑　immediately

❑　only when my lawyer releases the document to my attorney

❑　only when a medical doctor certifies I am no longer competent to manage my own financial affairs

OTHER

If allowed by your provincial legislation, do you want to name someone to monitor, or oversee, the financial decisions your attorney or representative makes on your behalf?

Yes   *No*

❏   ❏   I've chosen my representative with care.

If yes, who would you like to monitor, or oversee these decisions?

Name _____ Address _____

Name _____ Address _____

Do the people you have appointed in your pre-estate document for financial matters know where to find:

Yes   *No*

❏   ❏   the original document that names them?

❏   ❏   the details of your financial life (such as recorded on the forms in this workbook)?

FOR PERSONAL AND HEALTH CARE

In addition to the power of attorney document for financial decisions, most Canadians are also able to prepare a document appointing someone of their own choosing to make personal and health care decisions on their behalf, in the event they become unable to make these decisions on their own behalf. The decisions related to personal care could include where you will live, what you will wear, who you see, and what you eat. The decisions related to medical care range from consenting to medical tests and major surgery, to withholding medical treatment.

While you are not required to name someone to make these decisions, naming a power of attorney means that someone of your choice—not a government official—has the right to make personal care and health care decisions for you when you can't. However, immediate family members may be able to make certain health care decisions on your behalf in medical emergencies, even without this document.

Some provincial legislation also covers advanced health care directives, which are sometimes referred to as living wills, regarding advanced medical care that can be included in this pre-estate document. Some provinces have legislation that covers health care and advanced health care directives; others also cover personal care. And the legislation across the county continues to evolve.

In most provinces, this document is a separate document from the power of attorney for financial matters. Even in provinces where they can be combined, many lawyers prepare two separate documents, for your added privacy. Some lawyers include the advanced health care directives or the living will in the document for personal and health care, others prepare a separate living will.

Unlike a general power of attorney for finances, the document for personal and health care decisions generally is not effective until you become incapable of making these decisions for yourself.

The person you appoint is referred to by different names, depending on the province in which you live. This person may be called a health care proxy, representative, or a power of attorney for personal care. See the following chart for the term used in your province.

Who's Who for Personal and Health Care Directives

	Name of Representative	Name of Document
Alberta	agent	Personal Directive
British Columbia	representative	Representative Agreement for Health Care
Manitoba	proxy	Health Care Directive
New Brunswick	attorney for personal care	Power of Attorney for Personal Care
Newfoundland	substitute decision-maker	Advance Health Care Directive
Nova Scotia	deemed guardian	Authorization to Give Medical Consent
Ontario	attorney	Continuing Power of Attorney for Personal Care
Quebec	mandatary	Mandate Given in Anticipation of Incapacity
Prince Edward Island	proxy	Health Care Directive
Saskatchewan	proxy	Health Care Directive

You'll find a list of the duties of a power of attorney or representative for personal and health care decisions in Appendix C.

SAMPLE POWER OF ATTORNEY DOCUMENT
FOR PERSONAL AND HEALTH CARE DECISIONS

In this section, I've used the terms from the province of Ontario and refer to your substitute decision-maker for personal and health care as your attorney.

---

1. Introduction

This is a Power of Attorney for Personal Care made in accordance with s.46(s) of the *Substitute Decisions Act, 1992, S.O. 1992 c. 30.*

This Power of Attorney is given by Terri Ellis in the City of Toronto and Province of Ontario.

This section identifies the individual preparing the power of attorney for personal care by their full, proper name.

To prepare a power of attorney for health care or a living will, you must be mentally competent and in most provinces, be at least 16 years old.

2. Revocation

I revoke all former Powers of Attorney for Personal Care, including any living will.

The revocation clause states that this new power of attorney document for personal care revokes all previous power of attorney documents, as well as any related documents, such as a living will.

Destroying the original and all copies of a power of attorney of personal care also revokes it.

3. Appointment

I appoint my husband, Thomas Ellis, in the City of Toronto and the Province of Ontario, to be my Attorney for Personal Care in accordance with the *Substitute Decisions Act* to make decisions on my behalf with respect to my personal care if I am incapable of personal care decisions.

The person you appoint as your power of attorney for personal or health care is only called upon when, and if, you become incapable of making your own decisions on these matters, or if he or she reasonably believes you are no longer capable of making a required medical decision yourself. They do not have to be a lawyer.

Some people appoint the same person as their decision-maker for the financial decisions as well as for their personal and health care decisions, although you can appoint different people. The person you appoint should be someone you trust, who understands your personal values, and will follow your instructions or, if you have not left detailed instructions, will make decisions based on what he or she believes is in your best interest and will stand up for your wishes. Talking to your attorney ahead of time and letting him or her know your wishes would provide some guidance.

This sample is provided for illustration only. Not to be copied.

Some provinces prevent certain people from acting as your representative for personal or medical care, to reduce the possibility of abuse. For example, you may not be able to appoint your doctor, nurse, social worker, or landlord to make these decisions on your behalf unless he or she is also your spouse.

If you appoint more than one person to act as your attorney, they are required to make decisions on your behalf together, unless you state that they may act jointly and severally, that is, they can make decisions together or act independently.

In some provinces, such as British Columbia, residents can, if they want, name a monitor who will monitor the actions of their named representative to determine whether or not they are performing their duties.

4. Substitution

In the event that the above appointed Attorney is unable to act by reason or death, becoming incapacitated or resignation, I substitute and appoint my sisters, Cathie Scott and Diane Logan acting together, to be my Attorneys for Personal Care in accordance with the *Substitute Decisions Act* and to do on my behalf anything that I can lawfully do by an Attorney for personal care; including my health care, nutrition, shelter, clothing, hygiene, and safety, without limiting the generality of the foregoing, the elements of personal care referred to in s.45 and s.59(2) of the *Substitute Decisions Act*.

It's a good idea to include the name of a substitute or backup attorney, who is willing and able to act on your behalf in the event the original cannot when the time comes.

If your first choice becomes unwilling or unable to act, or unable to continue to act, and you don't name an alternate or backup attorney, your power of attorney document could be revoked. Then the decision-maker of last resort—someone from the office of the provincial public guardian and trustee—would make or oversee the decisions made on your behalf.

5. Powers

a) In the event my capacity for personal care is in issue and an assessment of my capacity is required, any physician selected by my attorney shall perform such assessment.

b) I authorize my Attorney(s) to make any personal care decisions for me that I am mentally incapable of making for myself, including health care, nutrition, shelter, clothing, hygiene, and safety, without limiting the generality of the foregoing, as well as the giving or refusing of consent for treatment to which the *Health Care Consent Act* applies.

c) To sign, execute, deliver, acknowledge, and make declaration in any documents needed to exercise any of the powers granted in this Power of Attorney document, as well as pay reasonable compensation or costs in the exercise of such powers.

Unless restrictions are specified, a power of attorney document authorizes your attorney to act on your behalf for all personal and health care decisions, including selecting a physician to determine whether or not you are mentally capable to make these decisions yourself.

This sample is provided for illustration only. Not to be copied.

Your representative does not have to make exactly the same decisions you would make if you were able; they only have to make decisions that are in your best interest. Of course, it could help your representative(s) if you discuss your wishes with them while you are mentally capable.

This document provides the attorney with the power to take legal action on your behalf related to the power of attorney for health care and the consent or right to refuse treatment.

---

d) Giving or Refusing Consent to Treatment

The following are my instructions to my Attorney, and my wishes, with respect to the giving or refusing of consent to specified kinds of treatment under specified circumstances: I do not wish to have my life unduly prolonged by any course of treatment or any other medical procedure which prolongs my life only and which offers no reasonable expectation of my recovery from chronic or life threatening physical or mental incapacity, except as may be necessary for the relief of suffering and pain, and includes use of respiratory ventilation to assist breathing if I will not be able to breathe on my own, and artificial feeding through tube, intravenous or central line, other than for basic hydration.

As long as you are mentally competent, you have the right to refuse medical treatment but once you are mentally incapable, you are assumed to have given consent to all medical treatment considered necessary, unless you have an advanced care directive that states otherwise.

Your advanced health care directive (or your living will) indicates your wishes regarding the types or degree of health care or medical intervention you would like to receive or refuse when you are unable to speak for yourself. The more clearly you indicate your wishes, the easier it will be for your health care providers to follow your wishes in the spirit you intended. While the clauses can be very detailed, some people give their decision-maker the discretion to do what appears best, given the treatments available.

Some people include wording similar to "If it is anticipated that I cannot enjoy a reasonable quality of life after recovery or remission, I request that I be allowed to die and not be kept alive by artificial means or heroic measures."

---

7. Indemnification

I indemnify from any liability to me, my estate, or any third party, any person who, in reliance on this Power of Attorney, acts so as to carry out or act consistently with my wishes expressed herein and who in so doing does not act in a manner that such person considers is in my best interests.

The indemnification clause provides your power of attorney with the assurance that, if they act in your best interest and in good faith, they do not have to worry that they would be sued by you in the future (should you regain capacity), your estate, or anyone else who may have relied on instructions from the attorney.

This sample is provided for illustration only. Not to be copied.

8. Declarations

a) In making this Power of Attorney, I am aware that my Attorney has a genuine concern for my welfare and that in the future I may need my Attorney to make personal care decisions for me.

b) I hereby expressly declare and indicate that I have been made aware of the *Substitute Decisions Act* and the *Consent to Treatment Act*, and pursuant to said statutes, it is my wish and desire to appoint Thomas Ellis, as my Attorney for the purposes of making health care decisions for me in the event that I become incapable of acting independently.

c) I confirm that I am at least sixteen (16) years of age and that the attorney appointed herein for my personal care is also at least sixteen (16) years old.

d) Death is as much a reality as birth, growth, maturity, and old age. It is the one certainty of life. If the time should come when I can no longer take part in the decisions for my own future, I hereby direct that this statement be allowed to stand as an expression of my wishes made while I am mentally competent.

If the situation should arise where my attending physician(s) has determined that there can be no recovery by me from a physical and/or mental disability and that my death is imminent, I hereby direct that I be allowed to die. It is my desire not to be kept alive by artificial means or heroic measures which would only serve to artificially prolong the process of dying. I do not fear death itself as much as the indignities of deterioration, dependence, and endless pain. I request that I be allowed to die naturally with only the administration of medication and the performance of any medical procedures deemed necessary to provide me with comfort and/or to alleviate suffering, even though this may hasten the moment of my death.

This request is made after careful consideration. It may appear to place a heavy responsibility on those individuals whose care I am in. However, it is with the intention of relieving you of such responsibility and placing it wholly upon myself in accordance with my strong personal convictions that this statement is made.

Some of the declarations in the power of attorney for health care are required by provincial legislation; others are your personal statement of wishes and beliefs.

9. Signing Formalities

I have signed this Power of Attorney in the presence of both of the witnesses whose names appear below on this 21st day of January, 2002.

Terri Ellis

Terri Ellis

We are the witnesses to this Power of Attorney. We have signed this Power of Attorney in the presence of the person whose name appears above, and in the presence of each other, on the date shown above.

Neither one of us is the Attorney, a spouse or partner of the Attorney, a child of the grantor or person whom the grantor has demonstrated an intention to treat as a child of the grantor, or is less than eighteen (18) years old.

This sample is provided for illustration only. Not to be copied.

We have no reason to believe that the grantor is incapable of giving a Power of Attorney for Personal Care or making decisions in respect of which instructions are contained in this Power of Attorney.

_____   _____
(signature of witness)   (signature of witness)

_____   _____
(address)   (address)

_____   _____
(occupation)   (occupation)

The power of attorney must be executed properly. The person giving the power of attorney must sign the document in the presence of two competent adults. As well, the testator and the two witnesses normally initial the bottom of all the pages. The legislation in your province may require the person(s) you have appointed to provide their written consent.

Anyone named in the document as an attorney or alternative attorney, or employed as a paid caregiver, should not act as a witness.

PERSONAL AND HEALTH CARE WORKSHEET

This worksheet is designed to help you reflect on what you want to include in your power of attorney for personal or health care, whether you are preparing the document for the first time, or updating it. Some people may have a separate living will; others now include their living will instructions in their personal and health care document.

This worksheet is *not* a legal document.

APPOINTMENT

Yes   *No*

❑   ❑   Do you want your spouse or common-law partner to make personal and health care decisions alone on your behalf?
If not, who would you like to make personal and health decisions on your behalf?

Name _____ Address _____

Name _____ Address _____

Name _____ Address _____

Who would you like to act as your alternate, or backup decision-maker, if the above are unable or unwilling to do the job when the time comes?

Name _____ Address _____

Name _____ Address _____

Name _____ Address _____

Yes   *No*

❑   ❑   Have they agreed to act as your attorney(s)?

If you are naming more than one person to act on your behalf, do you want them to make:

Yes   *No*

❑   ❑   all decisions together?

❑   ❑   decisions together or separately?

DECISIONS YOU WANT YOUR ATTORNEY TO MAKE ON YOUR BEHALF

What decisions do you want your attorney to make on your behalf?

Personal Care

Yes	No	
❏	❏	where you will live. This might include moving out of your home and into an assisted-living or long-term care facility.
❏	❏	what you will wear
❏	❏	who may visit with you
❏	❏	what you will eat. This might require appointing someone who understands your dietary restrictions or observances.

Medical Care

Yes	No	
❏	❏	arranging regular medical and dental check-ups
❏	❏	consenting to medical tests, including exploratory surgery
❏	❏	consenting to major surgery
❏	❏	arranging palliative care
❏	❏	withholding medical treatment you might not want
❏	❏	participating in medical research studies or experimental treatments
❏	❏	releasing information related to your medical records and history
❏	❏	prohibiting prolonging of your life if there is no reasonable expectation of recovery, such as during the terminal stages of a terminal illness
❏	❏	releasing information related to your medical records and history

COMPENSATION

In addition to reimbursement for all reasonable out-of-pocket expenses related to looking after my personal and health care, I want my representative or attorney to receive:

❏ compensation that is equitable, given the amount of time and expertise required

❏ the sum of $_____ annually

❏ compensation according to the provincial fee scale. In some provinces, this is nil.

❏ nothing

EFFECTIVE DATE

I would like this document for personal and health care to become effective:

❏   immediately

❏   only when it is reasonable to assume I am no longer able to make my own personal and health care decisions

OTHER

If allowed by your provincial legislation, do you want to name someone to monitor, or oversee, the personal and health care decisions your attorney or representative makes on your behalf?

Yes   *No*

❏   ❏   If yes, who would you like to monitor, or oversee these decisions?

Name _____   Address _____

Name _____   Address _____

Do the people you have appointed in your pre-estate document for personal and health care know where to find:

Yes   *No*

❏   ❏   the original document that names them?

❏   ❏   your wishes regarding your personal and medical care?

Remember, this worksheet is designed to help you think through some of the items you want stated in your personal and health care document.

UPDATING YOUR PRE-ESTATE PLANNING DOCUMENTS

It's important to review your pre-estate documents to ensure they accurately document your wishes and the current legislation.

If you answer *yes* or *unsure* to any of the following questions, you need to update your power of attorney documents, which is usually accomplished by preparing and signing a new document..

Since your documents were prepared, have you:

Yes *No* *Unsure*
❑ ❑ ❑ married? remarried? divorced? been widowed?

❑ ❑ ❑ signed a marriage contract or co-habitation agreement?

❑ ❑ ❑ separated or divorced?

❑ ❑ ❑ increased/decreased your net worth significantly?

❑ ❑ ❑ moved to a new province or country?

❑ ❑ ❑ undergone significant changes in your health?

Have there been other changes that might affect these documents?

Yes *No* *Unsure*
❑ ❑ ❑ Has your province changed its legislation related to finance, personal and health care in the event of incapacity?

❑ ❑ ❑ Have there been any changes to family law in your province?

❑ ❑ ❑ Has your representative or attorney moved, become too old or ill to carry out the duties and responsibilities?

❑ ❑ ❑ Is your representative or attorney now unwilling to perform the duties?

CHAPTER THREE

Your Will

The Key Estate Planning Document

The will is the most basic estate planning document. It's what most people associate with estate planning, but it is by no means the only thing to consider or document when doing an estate plan. Nonetheless, the will is the cornerstone of your entire estate plan.

Your will has two main functions: firstly, to name your executor—the person who will have the authority to settle up your estate and secondly, to specify who gets what. These instructions do not become effective until after your death, which is why you need the pre-estate document we discussed in the previous chapter, as well as a will. Having an up-to-date will means your estate is settled according to your instructions and does not have to be settled by default using your province's intestacy rule.

Even if you have designated beneficiaries for your life insurance policies, segregated funds, employer pension plans, as well as your registered retirement savings plan (RRSP) and your registered retirement income fund (RRIF), and have registered your assets jointly with rights of survivorship, you still need a will. These arrangements do not cover what you would want to have done, if you and the beneficiary (or joint owner) die in a common disaster; nor do they name someone to be the guardian for young children. They also do not appoint an executor—your legal representative—to deal with Canada Customs and Revenue Agency, CPP/QPP, and your financial institutions to wrap up the details of your financial life.

Wills come in many different forms. There are handwritten wills, computer-generated wills, and wills prepared by a lawyer or notary. Even wills prepared by lawyers and notaries reflect the professionals' own style that they have developed over the years.

Your will can be prepared by a lawyer (or notary, if you live in British Columbia or Quebec) or yourself. Here are some of the key reasons for having a lawyer prepare your will. The lawyer can:

- provide you with legal advice regarding your entire estate plan—not just your will

- ensure the wording and clauses in your will are legally valid

- state whether or not you were in your "right mind" when the will was prepared

- ensure the will was signed and witnessed properly.

SAMPLE WILL

A will is made up of a number of different clauses that reflect your personal situation and the province you live in.

In the following section, I have provided a number of different clauses in boxes to illustrate some of the more common ones found in a will. The comments that follow provide a brief explanation of what each clause really means and some of its implications. These clauses should not be used to prepare your own will which will require clauses customized for your own province as well as some clauses that are not discussed here. I recommend you obtain personalized advice for your situation from your notary or lawyer regarding the wording to be used in your jurisdiction.

> ### 1. Identification of Testator
> This is the last Will and Testament of me, Robert Goderich, of the City of Toronto, and the Province of Ontario.

This section identifies the individual preparing the will by his or her full, proper name and contains a statement stating that this document is his or her last will and testament.

Letters probate or the certificate of appointment of the Estate Trustee are issued using this name. It should match the name used at your financial institutions.

If the will is being made in contemplation of marriage and you want to ensure that the marriage does not revoke the will, you'll need to state that the will was made in contemplation of marriage. Some lawyers also add that the fiancé(e) would not benefit under the will if the marriage does not take place.

To prepare a will, you must be mentally competent and have reached the age of majority in your province, or if you are under the age of majority, married or a mariner or a member of the armed forces.

> ### 2. Revocation
> I hereby revoke all previous Wills, Codicils and Testamentary Dispositions of every nature or kind made by me.

The revocation clause states that the new will revokes any previous will. It is found in almost every will, even in the first will you prepare. If you die with more than one will for the same assets, only the instructions in the most recent will are followed. There are situations where people have more than one will, for instance, one will for those assets that require probating and another for assets that do not.

In addition to preparing a new will, there are other events that might revoke or change certain clauses in your will, such as a divorce or a marriage after a will is prepared.

This sample is provided for illustration only. Not to be copied.

---

3. Executor and Trustee

I appoint my wife, Sonna Goderich, to be the sole Executor and Trustee of my Will.

I refer to the Executor and Trustee, or Executrix and Trustee, or Executors and Trustees, original or substituted or surviving as my "Estate Trustee."

The executor, or executrix if female, is the person you designate to carry out a long list of duties to wrap up your financial affairs and distribute your estate according to the instructions in your will. In some provinces, this role is referred to as your estate trustee.

On your death, all the assets registered in your name are transferred into your estate. This estate is sometimes referred to as a trust, and your estate trustee or executor acts as the trustee carrying out your instructions and distributing your estate to your beneficiaries. See Appendix A for a list of the executor's duties.

You can appoint one or more people, who have reached the age of majority, to act as your estate trustee(s), or you can appoint a corporate trustee, such as a trust company, or you can appoint a corporate trustee to act with a family member. If you name one person, then it is a good idea to name someone as an alternate or backup, in case your first choice is unwilling or unable to do the job when the time comes. But don't just assume they will be willing and able to act as your executor—ask them.

If you want to appoint more than one person, consider how you want them to resolve any disputes that may arise. If you want any disputes resolved by a majority vote, or some other method, it should also be documented in your will.

In some cases, your executor may also be named to be the trustee of any testamentary trusts being set up under your will, such as for young children or a spousal trust. Since these trusts may last much longer than the estate trust, consider whether or not your executor should be the trustee of these other trusts.

If my wife does not survive me, or becomes unwilling or unable to act or continue to act as my Executor and Estate Trustee before all trusts set out in my Will have been fully performed, I appoint my friend, Jack Martin, to be the sole Executor and Trustee of my Will in the place and stead.

If you name one person to be your executor, and he or she is unable or unwilling to act as your executor when the time comes, your beneficiaries will have to apply to the courts to have someone named in their place, unless you name an alternate or backup. Some people also name a backup to the backup.

This sample is provided for illustration only. Not to be copied.

4. Transfer of Property to Estate Trustee

a) I give all my property of every nature and kind, wherever it is, to my Estate Trustee upon the following trusts, namely:

Your assets are transferred to the estate trustee in trust for the payment of debts and taxes, and ultimately to be distributed according to the instructions in your will.

Your will does not distribute:

- assets dealt with under a marriage contract
- assets with a designated beneficiary, such as your RRSPs or RRIFs, employer pension plans, life insurance, etc., unless the beneficiary named is "estate"
- assets owned jointly with rights of survivorship
- business assets dealt with under a shareholders' agreement or buy-sell agreement
- income you receive from a trust, where that trust agreement states that the income ceases on your death. For example, you are receiving income from a spousal trust, set up according to the instruction in your late spouse's will, where the trust states that on your death any remaining assets are to be distributed to the children from his or her first marriage.
- assets held in a family trust or an alter ego trust.

When you are considering who gets what on your death, it makes a lot of sense to consider the distribution of all the assets in your estate, not just the assets that are distributed according to the instructions in your will. This will help ensure your estate ends up where you want it to.

b) Debts and Taxes

My Estate Trustee shall pay out of the capital of my estate all my just debts, including any income taxes payable for the year(s) prior to my death, and in the year of my death to the date of my death, funeral and testamentary expenses and all succession duties, estate, gift, inheritance and death taxes, whether imposed pursuant to the law as of this or any other jurisdiction, otherwise payable by any beneficiary under my Will or any Codicil or of any settlement made by me, by any beneficiary named by me in any life insurance, plan or contract owned by me, or by any donee of any gift made by me.

And I hereby authorize my Estate Trustee to commute or prepay any such taxes or duties. This direction shall not extend to or include any such taxes that may be payable by a purchaser or transferee upon or after my death pursuant to any agreement with respect to such property.

This clause gives your executor the legal authority to pay all your debts, taxes, fees, and administrative expenses, but you cannot avoid your debts by leaving out this clause.

This sample is provided for illustration only. Not to be copied.

---

c) Personal Property

To deliver all articles of personal and household use or ornament to my wife, Sonna Goderich, if she survives me, for her own use absolutely.

This clause would transfer all household contents to Robert's wife.

---

d) Memorandum

In the event that I prepare a memorandum to assist my Estate Trustee in connection with setting forth my wishes as to the disposition of articles of personal and household use or ornament, I hereby direct my Estate Trustee to be guided by my wishes and to pay, deliver, or transfer items pursuant to the instructions contained within the said memorandum so far as possible to give effect to such wishes and to exercise their discretion where necessary.

Some people prefer to list their personal items in a memorandum, rather than listing them all in the will. While the list may not be binding unless it is in the will, the memorandum can provide guidance to your executor and beneficiaries as a statement of your wishes.

---

e) Bequests

To deliver my gold pocket watch to my grandson, David Goderich, if he survives me.

You can use your will to distribute the assets by:

- bequesting a specific item
- giving cash
- holding assets in a testamentary trust, where the beneficiary has the right to receive the income and/or capital from the trust, until the assets are ultimately distributed.

A will might contain a number of specific bequests or it might contain none. If the property is real estate, it is referred to as "devising" rather than bequesting.

If you don't own the item at the time of your death, it will not be distributed. You may worry that if you bequest an item in your will it is no longer yours. But it is still yours to do with as you see fit, even sell it. But if you sell it and you still want that person to receive something, it may be time to update your will.

If the beneficiary is not alive at the time of your death, consider whether you want the item to be left to an alternate beneficiary, or to be distributed as part of the residue of your estate.

---

f) Cash Legacies and Charitable Bequests

To pay the sum of Ten Thousand Dollars ($10,000) to each of my nephews and nieces, that survive me.

This sample is provided for illustration only. Not to be copied.

To pay the sum of Fifteen Thousand Dollars ($15,000) to my housekeeper, Martha Mayhew, if she survives me.

To pay the sum of Ten Thousand Dollars ($10,000) to the University of Toronto for general purposes.

It's important to calculate the value of cash legacies in your will. In this example, if Robert has eight nieces and nephews, this one statement adds up to $80,000 in cash gifts.

What do you want to do with the gift if the person named is not alive at the time of your death? Consider whether you want the amount left to an alternate beneficiary, or if it should be distributed as part of the residue of your estate.

When making a gift to charity in your will, it's important to specify the name of the charity as well as the amount of the gift, or the formula to be used to determine the amount of the gift. If you leave the amount or the charity to the discretion of your executor, the tax receipt may be disallowed.

g) Residue

If my spouse, Sonna Goderich, survives me and is alive thirty (30) days after the date of my death, my Estate Trustee shall pay and transfer the residue of my estate to my spouse in trust.

If my spouse, Sonna Goderich, should predecease me or survive me, but die within a period of thirty (30) days following my death, my Estate Trustee shall divide the residue of my estate into five (5) equal shares to pay and deliver such shares as follows:

(i) to my daughter, Sarah Goderich, three (3) shares; if my daughter is not living at the date of my death, then divide that share in equal shares among her issue per stirpes

(ii) to my granddaughter, Lauren Goderich, one (1) share

(iii) to my grandson, David Goderich, one (1) share.

The residue is the value of your estate that remains after the taxes, debts, fees, and expenses have been paid and specific bequests and cash legacies have made. Every will should contain a residue clause to ensure that all assets of the estate have been distributed.

Older wills distributed much of an estate through bequests and cash gifts and then used the residue clause to distribute whatever was left over.

Today's wills tend to distribute the bulk of the estate using the residue clause, which can distribute your estate regardless of the final tax bill and its ultimate value, according to a formula or predetermined percentage.

This residue clause contains a survivorship clause (30 days). In the event that spouses or partners die close together, this clause enables their estates to be settled according to their respective wills, rather than making the assumption that the older of the two died first.

This sample is provided for illustration only. Not to be copied.

If any of the said children or grandchildren predecease me, and if any issue of such deceased persons should then be living, their share of the residue to which they would have been entitled if alive, shall be divided among the issue of the deceased then alive in equal shares per stirpes.

If any of the said children or grandchildren should leave no surviving issues, such share of the amount thereof remaining shall be divided by my Estate Trustee among my surviving issue, in equal shares per stirpes.

The instructions in your will should cover a number of what-ifs. In this example, if any of the testator's children or grandchildren are not alive at the time of his or her death, what would have been their inheritance will go to their children or grandchildren, if they are alive.

When an inheritance is left on a "per stirpes" basis, if the beneficiary (for instance, your adult child) predeceases you, the gift that would have been his or hers passes through the family line to the next generation (in this case, to your grandchildren).

Another what-if to consider is how would you want your estate distributed if you are not survived by any immediate family. Would you want your estate to go to charity, distant relatives, or close friends?

5. RRSP Contributions

I give my Estate Trustee the absolute discretion to make any contribution considered appropriate to any RRSP where I am an annuitant or the contributor, in the year of my death or sixty (60) days after my death.

If the deceased had unused RRSP contribution room and is survived by a spouse or a common-law spouse who is under 70 and still able to have an RRSP, the executor or personal representative can make a contribution to a spousal RRSP and get an additional deduction to reduce the final tax bill. The contribution must be made in the year of death, or by the following March 1st.

6. Powers of Estate Trustee

In order to carry out the trusts of my will, I give my Estate Trustee the following powers to be used in the exercise of an absolute discretion at any time:

The executor gets his or her authority from the will and his or her powers can be as broad and discretionary as you believe are necessary to enable your executor to deal with your creditors, beneficiaries, as well as protect, manage, and distribute the assets of your estate.

If the executor's powers are not specified in a will, they are defined and limited to those specified in your province's *Trustee Act.*

---

a) Investments

My Estate Trustee shall make any investments for my estate that my Estate Trustee considers appropriate, including units or other interest of any mutual funds, common trust funds, unit trusts, or similar investments, without being limited to those investments authorized by law for trustees. I specifically authorize my Estate Trustee(s) to invest in any mutual funds or pooled investments they consider appropriate.

My Estate Trustee shall not be liable for any loss that may happen to my estate as a result of any investment made by my Estate Trustee in good faith.

In some provinces, unless the investment powers are specified in the will, the executor may be limited to investments that are authorized in the provincial *Trustee Act*.

Some provinces have a list of allowable investments, that might include GICs, bank deposits, fixed income investments backed by the federal or provincial governments, and certain corporate bonds and shares.

Other provinces require the estate trustee to meet the "prudent investor standard of care," or the level of care a prudent investor would take when managing money. This means the trustee must consider a number of factors when managing the investment portfolio, including:

- general economic conditions
- the effect of inflation or deflation
- realistic return expectations for income and capital appreciation
- the purpose of any special asset in the trust
- the need for liquidity, income, and/or the preservation of capital, as well as
- tax consequences of the investment strategy

You could provide your executor with the complete discretion to select investments as he or she sees fit, or limit the types of investments.

---

b) Real Estate

I authorize my Estate Trustee(s) to sell, divide, exchange, or otherwise dispose of the whole or any part of my real property when and how, they in their discretion consider advisable. I give the Estate Trustee the power to execute and deliver any deed, mortgage, lease, or other instrument that may be necessary to complete such a sale, mortgage, lease, or other disposition. This power of sale is discretionary.

This clause would enable your Estate Trustee to sell, lease, subdivide, or even hold on to real estate in a down market and wait for the market value to recover.

---

c) Selling and Disposing

My Estate Trustee shall realize or dispose of any assets of my estate, subject to the trusts of my Will, in any manner and on any terms.

This clause enables your executor to hold on to or sell any assets in the trust.

---

d) Settlement of Claims

Without the consent of any person interested under my Will, my Estate Trustee may compromise, settle, or waive any claim at any time due to or by my estate, and may make any agreement with any person, government, or corporation which shall be binding upon all persons interested in my estate.

In the event your executor has to deal with any creditors, this clause gives your executor the power to settle any claims without requiring the approval of your beneficiaries.

---

e) Dealing with Securities

My Estate Trustee may deal with any securities, shares or other interests of any corporation that is held by my estate, to the same extent as if I were alive. My Estate Trustee may take up new or further shares or other interests, may join in any reorganization, may exchange shares or other interests, and may give or accept and exercise options. My Estate Trustee may pay out of my estate any money needed for any of these purposes.

The "of any corporation that is held in my estate" is key to this clause as it enables your estate trustee to make decisions regarding any corporate business interests you may have, such as an investment holding company or a privately-held active business.

---

f) Retain Agents

My Estate Trustee may appoint and retain any person (which includes a trust company or other corporation) as their agent and to delegate the administrative details of the management of the estate or any part of the estate to that agent, on the terms and conditions at my Estate Trustee's discretion, and to pay the fees of the agent as a proper administration charge of my estate. My Estate Trustee shall not be liable for any default, neglect, or omission of such agent, provided my Estate Trustee exercised reasonable care in the selection and supervision of such agent.

If your executor(s) does not have the time or the expertise to perform all the administrative functions, they should know that many trust companies provide administrative services that could help them settle your estate. Your executor is still responsible for fulfilling the executor duties.

This is not the same as appointing a new executor, which can only be done through the courts.

g) Employ Other Professionals

My Estate Trustee(s) may hire, and pay out of my estate, such professional advisors as my Estate Trustee(s) deem necessary in the discharge of their duties. They may act upon the opinion or advice of, or information obtained from any lawyer, accountant, financial adviser, broker, real estate agent, auctioneer, surveyor, valuer, life or fire insurance adviser, or other expert, and my Estate Trustee shall not be responsible for any loss resulting by so acting or not acting, as the case may be.

Some executors may be reluctant to hire professionals because they see it as spending the beneficiaries' money; some beneficiaries may not want the executor to hire professionals for the same reason.

If you want your executor(s) to be able to hire professionals to help protect the value of your estate, such as an accountant to calculate the minimum amount of tax due, or a real estate appraiser to ensure property is sold for a fair price, this clause authorizes them to pay for these services out of the estate.

h) Elections

My Estate Trustee may at any time make or choose not to make, any elections or designation, or may do or choose not to do, any other act or exercise any discretion or authority referred to in the *Income Tax Act*, which my Estate Trustee considers in the best interest of my estate and my beneficiaries.

This clause gives your estate trustee the authority to make last-minute elections to minimize your final tax bill based on the tax laws in effect at the time of your death.

You should also review your estate plan periodically to determine if there are any steps you should take, while you are alive, to minimize your final tax bill.

i) Transactions with Estate Trustee

In my Estate Trustee's personal capacity, Estate Trustee may purchase assets from my estate if the purchase price and other terms are unanimously approved by my Estate Trustee and by the adult beneficiaries of my estate. My Estate Trustee shall not be required to obtain the approval of any Court for such purchase.

This clause gives your executor the power to purchase assets out of the estate, without requiring court approval, as long as they have the approval of all adult beneficiaries.

j) Conversion of Assets

My Estate Trustee shall call in the assets of my estate and may sell the assets at such times, for such price, in such manner and upon such terms as my Estate Trustee(s), in exercising their absolute discretion, considers appropriate.

I authorize my Estate Trustee to hold any assets of my estate without liability for loss or depreciation for as long as my Estate Trustee in the exercise of an absolute discretion considers appropriate, whether or not it may not be an investment in which a trustee may, by law, invest trust funds.

This clause gives your executor the power to sell your assets as they see fit, and protects them from being liable to the beneficiaries for any losses that might be incurred if they decide to hold on to certain assets.

k) Limit of Liability

My Estate Trustee shall not be liable for any loss that may happen to the value of my estate or to any beneficiary named in my Will that results when my Estate Trustee(s) acted in good faith under the discretion given to them in my Will.

As long as your executor(s) acted in good faith, this clause releases them from potential liabilities that might arise.

However, your executor(s) could be held personally liable if they distribute assets and then don't have enough left to pay your final tax bill to the Canada Customs and Revenue Agency, or if they failed to deal with a spouse's rights under provincial family law.

l) Dispute Resolution

I give my Estate Trustee the power to retain the service of a mediator or arbitrator to resolve any disputes that may arise regarding any matters related to my estate and my Will.

While a carefully prepared estate plan can minimize the possibility of your estate being disputed, this clause specifically gives your executor the power to try to resolve any disputes that might arise without having to go to court.

By mediating estate disputes, rather than going to court, your estate can minimize the cost of resolving the dispute and help keep families from being torn apart.

Other powers you might give your executor could include the power to:

- distribute property "in specie" to the beneficiaries, that is, in kind rather than selling the asset and distributing cash to the beneficiaries
- deal with corporate or business assets and keep the business operating until it can be sold or wound up
- borrow money for the estate

This sample is provided for illustration only. Not to be copied.

7. Make Payments for Minors

I authorize my Estate Trustee to make payments or transfers for any person under the age of majority or otherwise under disability, to a parent or guardian or person acting as such person. The receipt of such parent or guardian or other person shall be a sufficient discharge to my Estate Trustee in respect of such payments.

A minor or a person who is mentally incapable cannot provide a legally binding receipt. This clause authorizes the Estate Trustee to accept a receipt for payment made out of the estate from their parent or legal guardian on their behalf.

8. Testamentary Trusts

a) Spousal Trust

My Estate Trustee shall hold the residue of my estate in trust for the lifetime of my spouse, Sonna Goderich. My Estate Trustee shall pay income to my spouse or use the income for her support, maintenance, and benefit from time to time, in such amounts out of the capital as my Estate Trustee(s), in exercising their absolute discretion, considers appropriate.

A spousal trust is a trust set up for the sole use of the spouse or common-law partner. Assets put into a spousal trust can be transferred in as if the assets had been left outright to the spouse, without triggering a tax bill, provided no one else can benefit from them as long as your spouse is alive.

Income earned in a spousal trust is taxed as a separate taxpayer at graduated tax rates and can provide an opportunity to continue to split income.

A trust can be set up in your will that does not take effect until after your death and can be used to manage assets and income for:

- children under the age of majority
- older children who are not yet ready for the responsibility of managing their inheritance
- people who are not able to take care of their own finances, due to illness, mental incapacity, or age
- providing ongoing support to one beneficiary, such as for your spouse or common-law partner. You can leave instructions in the trust for those assets to pass to another beneficiary or group of beneficiaries, such as your children from a previous marriage
- income splitting, since the trust could be taxed as a completely separate taxpayer.

In some wills, the trust details can require several paragraphs.

This sample is provided for illustration only. Not to be copied.

b) Trust for Family Members

To hold the sum of one hundred thousand dollars ($100,000) in trust for the benefit of my mother, Isabelle Goderich, during her lifetime, with the power to my Estate Trustee(s) in their absolute discretion to encroach, if necessary, on the capital for the benefit of my mother. Upon my mother's death, the balance remaining is to be paid and delivered to the Children's Wish Foundation.

This clause is an example of the beneficiary of a trust being given the right to benefit from the assets held in trust for the remainder of his or her life. On the death of the beneficiary, the remaining value of the assets in the trust are passed to another beneficiary, in this case, a registered charity.

Suppose you want your children to enjoy the family cottage for as long as they live. Rather than leaving the cottage outright to the children, some people set up a family trust that would, among other things, define the rules to determine who would be able to use the cottage, when, and how it would be maintained.

c) Trusts for Minor Beneficiaries

If any person should become entitled to any share in my estate before attaining the age of twenty-five (25) years of age, the share of such person and any income derived from that share shall be held and kept invested by my Estate Trustee(s), and the income and capital, or so much thereof as my Estate Trustee(s), in their absolute discretion, considers necessary or advisable, shall be used for the benefit of such person until he or she attains the age of twenty-five (25) years.

At a minimum, assets that might be left to underage children need to be held in trust for them until they reach the age of majority, and a trustee named to manage those assets on their behalf. Otherwise, the public trustee may step in to manage the inheritance until the children reach the age of majority.

If you are concerned about your children receiving their inheritance before they have acquired the financial wisdom to handle it, you can restrict their inheritance until they are older and wiser. Some parents restrict a lump-sum payment until the children reach age 23 or 25 and provide earlier access to the funds for education expenses. Some parents leave payments from the trust funds to the discretion of the trustee.

For each trust you might want to set up under the instructions in your will, you need to consider

- why a trust is required
- if the beneficiaries will be entitled to receive income as well as capital from the assets held in the trust
- if the trustee should be the same person as the trustee of the estate
- the powers the trustee needs to do the job you want them to do

- whether or not the trustee(s) are free to use their discretion when making decisions
- how long the trust will likely be in effect
- any compensation the trustee will receive
- when the trust would be wound up and the assets ultimately distributed, such as when the youngest beneficiary reaches a certain age, on the death of the beneficiary, or some other event.

9. Guardians

In the event my wife and I die before any child of mine has attained the age of majority, I appoint my brother, Michael Goderich to have custody of such child and act as the guardian of such child until they attain the age of majority.

Providing for underage children motivates many couples to prepare their first will, even though it may be difficult to figure out who to name as legal guardian. However, if you do not make your wishes known, this important job would go to whomever the public trustee names.

A legal guardian is someone who assumes the responsibility for the child's well-being until that child reaches the age of majority. The guardian you name is granted temporary guardianship for the children, and must apply to the courts to be granted legal guardianship.

It's also a good idea to name a backup or alternate guardian in case your first choice is unable or unwilling to do the job.

The person you name as the guardian of your children may be someone different from the trustee you name to manage any inheritance left to the children.

Also, consider if you want to make a gift to the person named as the guardian, such as a lump sum to buy a larger car or to pay for a housekeeper, in the event they are called upon to fulfill this role.

10. Distribution in Kind

My Estate Trustee may divide, set aside, or pay any share or interest in some or all of the assets of my estate at the time of my death or at the time of division. My Estate Trustee has the absolute discretion to value the assets of the estate for the purposes of making this division, setting aside, or payment.

You can choose to have your assets sold and the cash distributed to your beneficiaries, or you can authorize your Estate Trustee to distribute assets "in kind" of equal value. Suppose you have a car worth $10,000. If one of your beneficiaries was interested in that car, the executor could give them the car, rather than cash of the same value.

This sample is provided for illustration only. Not to be copied.

Another clause might give the beneficiaries the right to purchase an asset from the estate at its fair market value. Perhaps you would like to give your beneficiaries the right of refusal to purchase the family cottage from the estate, based on age or geographic proximity.

11. Definition of Relationships

Any reference in my Will to a person in terms of a relationship to another person determined by blood or marriage shall not include a person born outside of marriage, or a person who comes within the description traced through another person who was born outside marriage.

Any person born outside of marriage but whose parents subsequently married one another shall not be regarded as being a person born outside of marriage.

Any person who has been legally adopted shall be regarded as having been born in the marriage of his or her adopting parent.

This clause provides a definition of "relationship" to be used when considering the legal status of any potential beneficiary under the will. However, there are a variety of definitions across the country as to who is a dependent. Under the *Dependent Relief Act*, this clause does not release you from any obligations you had to anyone who was financially dependent on you when you died.

12. Exclusions from Net Family Property

I declare that the income, including capital gains, arising from any interest passing to a beneficiary under my Will shall be excluded from such beneficiary's net family property or from the value of the beneficiary's assets on the death, divorce, or separation of such beneficiary, pursuant to the *Family Law Act*.

All gifts made to a beneficiary shall be the separate property of my beneficiaries and shall not be deemed to be community property or be subject to any other matrimonial rights of the spouses of my beneficiaries and shall not be liable for the obligations for any such spouse or community. All such gifts shall not be subject to seizure for the payment of any debts of beneficiaries or their representatives while in the possession and control of my Estate Trustee.

The rules related to family law and matrimonial property vary greatly across the country. In some provinces, all gifts and inheritances belong only to the person who inherited them. In other provinces, gifts and inheritances become part of family property. In Ontario, for example, all inheritances and any increase in the value of inherited property can be exempted from family property, meaning in the event of divorce, its value is not included in the settlement, provided the inheritance had not been used to buy a family asset.

13. Funeral Wishes

It is my wish that my body be cremated and my ashes buried in the plot owned by my spouse and myself at (location) in the City of Toronto.

While the final responsibility for arranging your funeral lies with your executor, you can provide your executor and family with guidance regarding your wishes.

Because some wills are not located until days after death, you should not rely solely on putting your funeral instructions in your will. Be sure to tell your executor and those close to you what you would like regarding your funeral, burial, or cremation. Similarly, if you wish to be considered for organ or tissue donation, be sure to let the people close to you know, and complete your province's organ donor card.

If your executor considers your instructions to be inappropriate for whatever reason or too elaborate for what your estate can afford, he or she has the final say and can override your wishes.

14. Compensation

I authorize my Estate Trustee(s) to pay themselves from the income and/or capital of my estate reasonable compensation at reasonable intervals. If any compensation subsequently awarded by the Court or agreed to by the beneficiaries is less than the compensation taken by the Estate Trustee, the Estate Trustee will repay the difference to the estate.

Your executor has to do, or arrange to have done, everything from emptying out your refrigerator to dealing with Canada Customs and Revenue Agency on your behalf, and is consequently entitled to fair and reasonable compensation.

If the compensation, or a formula to be used to determine the compensation, is not specified in the will, the fee may have to be approved by the courts or by all of your beneficiaries.

As a rule of thumb, the maximum compensation is up to 5% of the total value of the estate. The actual amount of compensation allowed is related to the complexity of the estate, the types of assets or business interests your executor has to manage, the expertise required, as well as the time involved in settling the estate. You could also consider making a bequest to your executor, in lieu of or in addition to, paid compensation.

If you are appointing a trust company as your executor, the compensation you have negotiated with them should be documented in your will.

If any Estate Trustee(s) is a professional, they shall be entitled to compensation for acting as Estate Trustee, in addition to any reasonable fees for any other professional services they also provide.

This sample is provided for illustration only. Not to be copied.

If your executor is an accountant, lawyer, or other professional, or someone who provides services such as completing tax returns or legal advice, this clause enables them to be compensated for those services, in addition to receiving executor fees.

15. Governing Law

My will shall be governed by and construed in accordance with the laws of the Province of Ontario.

The will is normally governed by the laws of the province in which it was prepared—which should be where you normally live.

16. Signing Formalities

In testimony whereof I have to my Will, which is written upon this and the fifteen preceding pages, subscribed by my name this 21st day of January, 2002.

SIGNED, PUBLISHED, AND DECLARED   )
by the said Testator, Robert Goderich   )
as and for his last Will and Testament, in the   )
presence of us, both present at the same time,   )   *Robert Goderich*
who, at his request, in his presence and in the   )   Robert Goderich
presence of each other, have hereunto subscribed)
our names as witnesses.   )

_____
(signature of witness)

_____
(address)

_____
(occupation)

_____
(signature of witness)

_____
(address)

_____
(occupation)

To be properly executed, a formal will must be signed and witnessed. The testator's signature must be witnessed in the presence of two competent adults. The two witnesses also normally initial the bottom of all the pages.

Anyone named in the will as a beneficiary, spouse, trustee, or guardian, or married to anyone named as a beneficiary, trustee, or guardian, should not act as a witness. If they do, any inheritance they might have received could be ignored, since it raises concerns that they could have unduly influenced the testator.

If not done properly, something that seems as simple as signing a will, can cause your will to be invalid—this can easily happen with a do-it-yourself will. There have been cases where the courts have deemed a will to be invalid because the will did not have the required number of witnesses, or because the date the witnesses signed the will did not match the date the testator signed the will.

This sample is provided for illustration only. Not to be copied.

AFFIDAVIT OF EXECUTION

The courts may want to confirm that your will was properly executed before they will issue the court paperwork, commonly referred to a letters probate or a grant of probate. This would mean that your executor would have to locate your witnesses to obtain their formal statement.

To save time and expense after death, your lawyer may prepare an affidavit of execution and obtain a statement from each witness that the will was properly executed—that they indeed were in the room together and witnessed the testator signing the will.

SAMPLE AFFIDAVIT OF EXECUTION OF A WILL

AFFIDAVIT OF EXECUTION OF WILL

In the matter of execution of the will of Robert Goderich.

I, _____, of the City of Toronto in the Province of Ontario, make oath and say:

1. On the 21st day of January, 2002 I was present and saw the will written, annexed and marked as Exhibit "A" to this Affidavit executed by Robert Goderich.

2. At the time of execution I knew such person was over the age of eighteen years, to the best of my knowledge.

3. The said paper writing was executed by such person in the presence of myself, _____ and _____ (name of other witness) of the City of Toronto in the Province of Ontario.

We were both present at the same time, and witnessed and signed the document in the testator's presence.

Sworn before me in the City of Toronto in the Province of Ontario
this 21st day of January, 2002.

_____   _____
Commissioner of Oaths   Signature of Witness

This sample is provided for illustration only. Not to be copied.

WORKSHEETS FOR YOUR WILL

You have many choices in how you want the assets that flow into your estate to be distributed. In your will, you could provide for specific bequests or have your beneficiaries share in the residue after all your taxes and bills have been paid. You could provide that the inheritance be paid outright to the beneficiary or held in a trust on their behalf.

When considering how your estate will be distributed, you also need to consider the what-ifs of life. How do you want your estate to be distributed if any beneficiary is under the age of majority at the time of your death? What if a beneficiary predeceases you? What if you and your partner die in a common disaster?

While these what-ifs can be difficult to think about, considering what you want to have happen can ensure that your estate planning documents will reflect your wishes for as long as possible. As well, in the event you become mentally incapable of revising your will, you would want your existing will to be as good as it could be.

HOW DO YOU WANT YOUR ESTATE TO BE DISTRIBUTED?

Yes   *No*

❏   ❏   Do you want your entire estate to go to your spouse or partner?

If yes, do you want the estate to be distributed to your spouse or partner:

❏   Outright

❏   In trust. Reason for trust _____

❏   Some outright, some in trust

If no, how do you want your estate to be distributed?

_____

_____

If your spouse/partner does not survive you for more than 30 days, how do you want your estate to be distributed?

❏   As if your spouse/partner predeceased you?

❏   As if the older person died first?

Yes   *No*

❏   ❏   Do you want to make gifts of any personal items, family heirlooms, or sums of money to specific individuals or charities on your death?

If yes:

What or How Much	To Whom	When
_____	_____	_____
_____	_____	_____
_____	_____	_____
_____	_____	_____
_____	_____	_____

What or How Much	To Whom	When
_____	_____	_____
_____	_____	_____

Yes	No	
❑	❑	Have you provided for your spouse according to the family law or matrimonial property law in your province?
❑	❑	If you hold loans or mortgages for family members, do you want them to be forgiven on your death?

DISTRIBUTING THE RESIDUE OF YOUR ESTATE

The residue of your estate is the value of your estate after all your taxes and debts have been paid and any specific bequests have been made. Today, some people make the bulk of the distribution of the assets covered by their will through the residue clause to ensure that, regardless of the value of their estate, or the amount of taxes and other expenses, the residue will be distributed according to a pre-determined formula.

The residue can be left outright to your beneficiaries or held in a testamentary trust. A trust might be appropriate where assets need to be managed for minor children, for a relative who is not financially responsible, or for a beneficiary who has special needs. Testamentary trusts can also be useful to provide asset protection or creditor protection, privacy, or income splitting.

I want the residue of my estate to be distributed as follows:

Percentage of Residue	To whom	Outright	In Trust	Reason for Trust
_____	Spouse/Partner	❑	❑	_____
_____	Child _____	❑ at age_____	❑	_____
_____	Child _____	❑ at age_____	❑	_____
_____	Child _____	❑ at age_____	❑	_____
_____	Child _____	❑ at age_____	❑	_____
_____	Grandchild _____	❑ at age_____	❑	_____
_____	Grandchild _____	❑ at age_____	❑	_____
_____	Grandchild _____	❑ at age_____	❑	_____
_____	Grandchild _____	❑ at age_____	❑	_____
_____	Grandchild _____	❑ at age_____	❑	_____
_____	Charity _____	❑	❑	_____
_____	Others _____	❑	❑	_____

OBLIGATIONS FOR DEPENDENTS

Yes   *No*

❑   ❑   Have you provided for your dependents according to the *Dependent Relief Act* and/or your obligations to provide continuing support?

If yes: List the names of any people, in addition to your spouse and children, who are financially dependent on you (grandchild, brother, sister, parent, same-sex partner, common-law spouse, etc.) and the amount of support you provide annually.

Name	Relationship	Amount of Support Provided
_____	_____	_____
_____	_____	_____
_____	_____	_____
_____	_____	_____

CONTINGENCY PLANNING

If any person named in your will is not alive at the time of your death, what do you want done with the money or gift they might have received?

Name

_____   ❑ To their children/ grandchildren   ❑ To charity
                          ❑ To someone else _____   ❑ Distribute as part of my residue

_____   ❑ To their children/ grandchildren   ❑ To charity
                          ❑ To someone else _____   ❑ Distribute as part of my residue

_____   ❑ To their children/ grandchildren   ❑ To charity
                          ❑ To someone else _____   ❑ Distribute as part of my residue

If no one in your immediate family survives you, how do you want your estate to be distributed?

❑   To charity

❑   To distant relatives

❑   Doesn't matter (In which case, it could be distributed according to intestacy rules.)

❑   _____

CHOOSING YOUR EXECUTOR

Being an executor, estate trustee, or estate representative is a job. The person(s) taking on this job can be held personally liable for their actions and if they fail to pay the tax bill before distributing the assets of the estate, they personally could have to pay any outstanding taxes. You'll find a list of the duties and responsibilities of an executor in Appendix A of this workbook.

Yes	No	
❑	❑	Do you want your spouse or partner to be your executor?

If no, who would you like to be your executor(s)?

Name   Address

_____   _____

_____   _____

_____   _____

Yes	No	
❑	❑	Are they to act as co-executors?

Alternate or backup executor(s)

Name   Address

_____   _____

_____   _____

_____   _____

Consider if these people:

Yes	No	Unsure	
❑	❑	❑	are capable of managing the financial responsibilities of the estate
❑	❑	❑	are willing and able to accept the job
❑	❑	❑	have the time to do the job
❑	❑	❑	could handle the responsibilities fairly and objectively
❑	❑	❑	live in your province
❑	❑	❑	are likely to outlive you
❑	❑	❑	get along, if you are considering having them act as co-executors

You might be better off appointing a professional executor, such as a trust company, an accountant, or lawyer if:

Yes	No	
❑	❑	you anticipate struggles for control of assets or a business.
❑	❑	you don't know anyone who has the expertise to be your executor.
❑	❑	you don't know anyone who is willing to accept the job.
❑	❑	the assets will be held for a number of years after your death before they are distributed.
❑	❑	your financial and family affairs are complex.

If you are considering naming a professional executor(s) or trustee(s), here are some important questions to consider:

How many accounts does each trust officer personally handle? _____

How many times a year will they meet, and where? _____

Are they experienced in dealing with situations similar to yours? ❑ Yes   ❑ No

What investment strategy/philosophy will be used?_____

_____

How will it work if you want to name a family member as co-executor? ❑ Yes   ❑ No

What will it cost? _____

Are their fees competitive? ❑ Yes   ❑ No

EXECUTOR POWERS

Do you want your executor(s) to have powers to:

Yes	No	
❑	❑	distribute assets, in kind or as is, to beneficiaries (legally called "in specie")?
❑	❑	sell assets and pay cash to beneficiaries?
❑	❑	provide some funds to the beneficiaries before the estate is completely settled?
❑	❑	purchase assets of the estate?
❑	❑	make an RRSP contribution to a spousal RRSP?
❑	❑	pay taxes before the assets of the estate are distributed?
❑	❑	make elections under the *Income Tax Act* that would be beneficial to your estate, but are beyond the powers stated in the provincial *Trustee Act*?
❑	❑	invest as they see fit?
❑	❑	if your executor is a trust company, will you give them the power to invest in their own securities (such as mortgages they arrange)?
❑	❑	determine which assets, if any, are to be held in a spousal trust?
❑	❑	borrow on behalf of the estate?
❑	❑	purchase assets from the estate?
❑	❑	consult with or hire professionals, such as accountants, lawyers, professional trustees, or financial advisors, and to pay them from money in the estate?

COMPENSATION

All executors are entitled to receive compensation out of the estate of up to 5% of the value of the estate, depending on the time and expertise required to settle the assets in the estate.

I want my executor to receive:

❏   compensation that is equitable, given the amount of time and expertise required to settle my estate

❏   the sum of $ _____

❏   a bequest in my will other than cash

❏   nothing

OTHER

Does your executor know the location of your will?   ❏ Yes ❏ No

Does your executor know the location of this workbook? ❏ Yes ❏ No

CHOOSING A GUARDIAN

A major motivating factor for many people preparing their first will is "who will look after my children if I die before they become adults?" Your choice of their guardian, the person who will be responsible for the care of your child while they are minors, is not a minor consideration.

If your children could be young when you die, who do you want to act as their legal guardian?

Name _____   Address _____

Yes	No	Unsure	
❏	❏	❏	Is this person someone your children would want to live with?
❏	❏	❏	Is this person willing to assume the responsibilities of raising your children?
❏	❏	❏	Can this person afford to raise your children?
❏	❏	❏	Will you provide financial support for the children while they are in the guardian's care?
❏	❏	❏	Should this person be named as the trustee of the children's inheritance?

Some people name the same person to act as both their children's guardian and the trustee of the children's inheritance. But some people find that the loving and caring qualities they want in a guardian and the financial acumen they want in their the trustee, may not exist in the same person.

REVIEWING YOUR WILL

Nothing remains the same. Every few years, it's important to review your will to ensure it continues to document your wishes and the needs of your beneficiaries. Events that occur in your life could directly affect your estate plan. Your will needs to accurately reflect your wishes and your situation at the time of your death.

If you answer *yes* or *unsure* to any of the following questions, you may need to update your will.

If it took you years to get around to preparing your first will, don't take as long to get around to reviewing it!

WILL REVIEW CHECKLIST

Since your will was prepared, have you:

Yes	No	Unsure	
❏	❏	❏	married? remarried? divorced? been widowed?
❏	❏	❏	signed a marriage contract or co-habitation agreement?
❏	❏	❏	separated or divorced?
❏	❏	❏	started working?
❏	❏	❏	stopped working or retired?
❏	❏	❏	had or adopted a child?
❏	❏	❏	lost to death a child? or grandchild?
❏	❏	❏	been predeceased by any of your beneficiaries?
❏	❏	❏	gained any grandchildren?
❏	❏	❏	started an RESP?
❏	❏	❏	planned for how the assets in any in-trust-for accounts to are to be handled?
❏	❏	❏	added dependants? For example, are you now supporting aging parents or do you have children who have moved back home?
❏	❏	❏	loaned money to your children?
❏	❏	❏	had any children reach the age of majority?
❏	❏	❏	had any children marry? remarry? separate? enter a common-law relationship?
❏	❏	❏	increased/decreased your net worth significantly?

Yes	No	Unsure	
❑	❑	❑	bought a home or acquired property, such as a cottage?
❑	❑	❑	received an inheritance or significant gift?
❑	❑	❑	made a substantial gift?
❑	❑	❑	started a business?
❑	❑	❑	sold a business?
❑	❑	❑	bought life insurance?
❑	❑	❑	started a retirement plan? RRSP? a pension?
❑	❑	❑	moved to a new province or country?
❑	❑	❑	decided to add/remove a beneficiary for your registered retirement plans, pension plan or life insurance?
❑	❑	❑	started to receive income from a trust?
❑	❑	❑	thought about setting up a trust?
❑	❑	❑	thought about making a planned gift?

Since your will was prepared, have there been other changes that might affect your estate plan?

Yes	No	Unsure	
❑	❑	❑	Have the tax rules changed?
❑	❑	❑	Has your province changed its legislation related to finance, personal and health care in the event of incapacity?
❑	❑	❑	Have there been any changes to family law in your province?
❑	❑	❑	Has your executor or estate trustee moved, become too old or ill to carry out your wishes?
❑	❑	❑	Is your executor now unwilling or unable to perform the duties of executor?
❑	❑	❑	Has the person named as guardian moved, or is he or she now unwilling or unable to perform the duties of a guardian?
❑	❑	❑	Will your liabilities on death be greater than the value of your liquid assets?

UPDATING YOUR WILL

As much as I would like to be able to suggest you only have to prepare one will, if you are like many people, you will have to update your final instructions as your circumstances change. As you noticed when you completed the previous checklist, there are many life events that could affect your estate plan—and many legislative and tax changes that could also affect it.

There are two ways to update the instructions in your will. You could prepare:

• a completely new will

• a formal amendment, called a codicil, to an existing will

If the changes are simple, such as changing the person appointed to act as your trustee or as the guardian of your children, a codicil can be used to effectively and clearly indicate the change.

If there are a number of changes, preparing a completely new will makes your instructions easier to understand and follow.

A SAMPLE CODICIL

1. Introduction

This is a codicil to my Will dated 21st of January, 2002, of Robert Goderich, of the City of Toronto, in the province of Ontario.

If there is more than one codicil, each codicil would be referred to by number. For example, if a codicil was prepared last year, and you are preparing a subsequent one, the introduction would introduce this new codicil as the second one.

If you get to the point where you have more than one codicil, your instructions could become confusing and it may be better to prepare an entirely new will to avoid confusion. After all, you want your instructions to be easy to follow.

Just as you must be mentally competent to prepare a will, you must also be mentally competent to prepare a codicil to amend your will.

2. Revoking and Adding Clauses to the Will

a) I revoke the appointment of my brother, Michael Goderich, as the guardian of any minor child and appoint my sister, Cathie Goderich, in his place as guardian.

b) I confirm all other aspects of my Will.

In addition to adding certain clauses to your will, or revoking certain appointments and appointing others in their place, the codicil also contains a statement that you confirm all other aspects of your will.

3. Signing Formalities

In testimony whereof I have, to this Codicil to my Will, written upon this page, subscribed by my name this 21st day of February, 2002.

SIGNED, PUBLISHED, AND DECLARED)
by the said Testator, Robert Goderich)
as a Codicil to his Will, in the presence of us,)
both present at the same time, who at his)
request, in his presence and in the presence)
of each other, have hereunto subscribed our)
names as witnesses.)

Robert Goderich
Robert Goderich

_____
(signature of witness)

_____
(signature of witness)

This sample is provided for illustration only. Not to be copied.

_____   _____
(address)   (address)

_____   _____
(occupation)   (occupation)

The signing formalities for a codicil are the same as for the will, although the witnesses do not need to be the same people who witnessed the original will.

The Who's Who of Your Estate Plan

In this section, you'll find worksheets to record all the players of your estate plan, including:

- your own personal information
- the members of your family and where they are now
- your key professional and personal advisors
- the contact information for all the people named in your pre-estate and estate planning documents—your executor, representatives, trustee, guardians, etc.—the people you want to act on your behalf,

While some people think first about their assets when preparing an estate plan, the planning is really about the people in your life.

In the next two chapters, you'll find worksheets to list your assets and liabilities and where to find all of your important papers.

YOUR PERSONAL INFORMATION

Name: _____

Legal name (if different) : _____

Also known as: _____

Address: _____

City/Province/Postal code: _____

Home phone number: _____ Wireless cell/Pager #: _____

E-mail: _____

Place of birth: _____ Date of birth: _____

Citizenship: _____

Occupation: _____

Current employer: _____

Address of current employer: _____

Employer phone number: _____ Fax: _____

YOUR FAMILY

This may not be the easiest worksheet to complete, particularly if you're not great with birth dates. However, this snapshot of your family paints a picture of your family that can help your professional advisors and your executors locate the people in your life, regardless of whether or not they play an active role in it.

Marital Status

❏ Single ❏ Married ❏ Common-Law Spouse ❏ Same Sex

❏ Fiancée ❏ Divorced ❏ Separated ❏ Widowed

❏ Other: _____

Has your partner been married before? ❏ Yes ❏ No

Spouse

Name: _____ Date of marriage:_____

Date of birth: _____ Place of birth: _____ Citizenship:_____

Occupation: _____ Special needs? _____

Common-Law Spouse

Name: _____ Date of co-habitation:_____

Date of birth: _____ Place of birth: _____ Citizenship:_____

Occupation: _____ Special needs? _____

Same-Sex Partner

Name: _____ Date of co-habitation:_____

Date of birth: _____ Place of birth: _____ Citizenship:_____

Occupation: _____ Special needs? _____

Ex-Partner

❏ Separated ❏ Divorced ❏ Other: _____

Name: _____

Date of birth: _____ Place of birth: _____ Citizenship:_____

Address of ex-spouse: _____ Phone no.: _____

Date of separation: _____ Separation agreement? ❏ Yes ❏ No

Date of divorce: _____

Support obligations? ❑ Yes ❑ No Amount: $_____   Continue after death? ❑ Yes ❑ No

Occupation: _____   Special needs?_____

Widowed

Name: _____

Date of spouse's death: _____ Estate settled? ❑ Yes ❑ No

Do any assets remain registered in spouse's name? ❑ Yes ❑ No

Children

Name: _____ Date of birth: _____

Name of other parent: _____ Citizenship: _____

Occupation: _____ Marital status: _____

Living with you: ❑ No ❑ Yes   If no, address _____

Financially dependent? ❑ No ❑ Yes $_____ /yr   Special needs?_____

Name: _____ Date of birth: _____

Name of other parent: _____ Citizenship: _____

Occupation: _____ Marital status: _____

Living with you: ❑ No ❑ Yes   If no, address _____

Financially dependent? ❑ No ❑ Yes $_____ /yr   Special needs?_____

Name: _____ Date of birth: _____

Name of other parent: _____ Citizenship: _____

Occupation: _____ Marital status: _____

Living with you: ❑ No ❑ Yes   If no, address _____

Financially dependent? ❑ No ❑ Yes $_____ /yr   Special needs?_____

Name: _____ Date of birth: _____

Name of other parent: _____ Citizenship: _____

Occupation: _____ Marital status: _____

Living with you: ❏ No ❏ Yes   If no, address _____

Financially dependent? ❏ No ❏ Yes $ _____ /yr   Special needs?_____

Name: _____ Date of birth: _____

Name of other parent: _____ Citizenship: _____

Occupation: _____ Marital status: _____

Living with you: ❏ No ❏ Yes   If no, address _____

Financially dependent? ❏ No ❏ Yes $ _____ /yr   Special needs?_____

Are any children adopted?
❏ No ❏ Yes   Names: _____

Other Relatives/Dependents

❏ Grandchild   ❏ Great-grandchild   ❏ Parents

❏ In-laws   ❏ Niece/Nephew   ❏ Other: _____

Name:_____ Date of birth: _____

Names of parents: _____ Citizenship: _____

Occupation: _____ Marital status: _____

Living with you: ❏ No ❏ Yes   If no, address _____

Financially dependent? ❏ No ❏ Yes $ _____ /yr   Special needs?_____

Note: Photocopy if more space is required.

❏ Grandchild   ❏ Great-grandchild   ❏ Parents

❏ In-laws   ❏ Niece/Nephew   ❏ Other: _____

Name:_____Date of birth: _____

Names of parents: _____Citizenship: _____

Occupation: _____Marital status: _____

Living with you: ❏ No ❏ Yes   If no, address _____

Financially dependent? ❏ No ❏ Yes $_____/yr   Special needs?_____

❏ Grandchild   ❏ Great-grandchild   ❏ Parents

❏ In-laws   ❏ Niece/Nephew   ❏ Other: _____

Name:_____Date of birth: _____

Names of parents: _____Citizenship: _____

Occupation: _____Marital status: _____

Living with you: ❏ No ❏ Yes   If no, address _____

Financially dependent? ❏ No ❏ Yes $_____/yr   Special needs?_____

❏ Grandchild   ❏ Great-grandchild   ❏ Parents

❏ In-laws   ❏ Niece/Nephew   ❏ Other: _____

Name:_____Date of birth: _____

Names of parents: _____Citizenship: _____

Occupation: _____Marital status: _____

Living with you: ❏ No ❏ Yes   If no, address _____

Financially dependent? ❏ No ❏ Yes $_____/yr   Special needs?_____

❑ Grandchild   ❑ Great-grandchild   ❑ Parents

❑ In-laws   ❑ Niece/Nephew   ❑ Other: _____

Name:_____ Date of birth: _____

Names of parents: _____ Citizenship: _____

Occupation: _____ Marital status: _____

Living with you: ❑ No   ❑ Yes   If no, address _____

Financially dependent? ❑ No   ❑ Yes $ _____ /yr   Special needs?_____

❑ Grandchild   ❑ Great-grandchild   ❑ Parents

❑ In-laws   ❑ Niece/Nephew   ❑ Other: _____

Name:_____ Date of birth: _____

Names of parents: _____ Citizenship: _____

Occupation: _____ Marital status: _____

Living with you: ❑ No   ❑ Yes   If no, address _____

Financially dependent? ❑ No   ❑ Yes $ _____ /yr   Special needs?_____

❑ Grandchild   ❑ Great-grandchild   ❑ Parents

❑ In-laws   ❑ Niece/Nephew   ❑ Other: _____

Name:_____ Date of birth: _____

Names of parents: _____ Citizenship: _____

Occupation: _____ Marital status: _____

Living with you: ❑ No   ❑ Yes   If no, address _____

Financially dependent? ❑ No   ❑ Yes $ _____ /yr   Special needs?_____

**Note:* Photocopy if more space is required.

YOUR PROFESSIONAL ADVISORS

List those people who provide you with professional advice. They could provide valuable information and guidance to your representatives and family.

Accountant

Name: _____

Address: _____

Phone: _____ Fax: _____

E-mail: _____

Bank Manager

Name: _____

Address: _____

Phone: _____ Fax: _____

E-mail: _____

Dentist

Name: _____

Address: _____

Phone: _____ Fax: _____

E-mail: _____

Family Doctor

Name: _____

Address: _____

Phone: _____ Fax: _____

E-mail: _____

Other Health Care Professional

Name: _____

Address: _____

Phone: _____ Fax: _____

E-mail: _____

Financial Advisor/Planner

Name: _____

Address: _____

Phone: _____ Fax: _____

E-mail: _____

Funeral Home/Director

Name: _____

Address: _____

Phone: _____ Fax: _____

E-mail: _____

Insurance Agent

Name: _____

Address: _____

Phone: _____ Fax: _____

E-mail: _____

Investment Advisor/Stockbroker

Name: _____

Address: _____

Phone: _____ Fax: _____

E-mail: _____

Lawyer

Name: _____

Address: _____

Phone: _____ Fax: _____

E-mail: _____

Minister/Priest/Rabbi/Other Clergy

Name: _____

Address: _____

Phone: _____ Fax: _____

E-mail: _____

Relative

Name: _____

Address: _____

Phone: _____ Fax: _____

E-mail: _____

Trust Officer

Name: _____

Address: _____

Phone: _____ Fax: _____

E-mail: _____

Other:

Name: _____

Address: _____

Phone: _____ Fax: _____

E-mail: _____

THE PEOPLE NAMED IN YOUR ESTATE PLANNING DOCUMENTS

Keeping the contact information for all the people you've named in your pre-estate planning documents for financial decisions and personal and health care decisions, as well as your will, provides valuable information to your family and friends. Complete all the sections below that apply to your personal situation. Feel free to photocopy this section for your spouse/partner or other members of your immediate family.

YOUR REPRESENTATIVE(S) FOR FINANCIAL DECISIONS

Representative(s)/Power of Attorney(s)/Mandate(s)/Representative

Yes   *No*

❑   ❑   Same as Estate Trustee(s)/Executor(s)

If no:

Name: _____

Address: _____

Phone: _____ Fax: _____

E-mail: _____

Name: _____

Address: _____

Phone: _____ Fax: _____

E-mail: _____

Backup(s):

Name: _____

Address: _____

Phone: _____ Fax: _____

E-mail: _____

Name: _____

Address: _____

Phone: _____ Fax: _____

E-mail: _____

Name: _____

Address: _____

Phone: _____ Fax: _____

E-mail: _____

YOUR REPRESENTATIVES FOR PERSONAL AND HEALTH CARE DECISIONS

Representative(s)/Power of Attorney(s)/Mandate(s)

Yes   *No*
❑   ❑   Same as Executor(s)/Estate Trustee(s)

If no:

Name: _____

Address: _____

Phone: _____ Fax: _____

E-mail: _____

Name: _____

Address: _____

Phone: _____ Fax: _____

E-mail: _____

Name: _____

Address: _____

Phone: _____ Fax: _____

E-mail: _____

Backup(s):

Name: _____

Address: _____

Phone: _____　Fax: _____

E-mail: _____

Name: _____

Address: _____

Phone: _____　Fax: _____

E-mail: _____

YOUR WILL

Executor(s)/Estate Trustee(s)

Name: _____

Address: _____

Phone: _____　Fax: _____

E-mail: _____

Name: _____

Address: _____

Phone: _____　Fax: _____

E-mail: _____

Backup Executor(s)/Estate Trustee(s)

Name: _____

Address: _____

Phone: _____　Fax: _____

E-mail: _____

Name: _____

Address: _____

Phone: _____ Fax: _____

E-mail: _____

Guardian(s)

❏ Same as Executor(s)/Estate Trustee(s)

Name: _____

Address: _____

Phone: _____ Fax: _____

E-mail: _____

Name: _____

Address: _____

Phone: _____ Fax: _____

E-mail: _____

Backup Guardian

Name: _____

Address: _____

Phone: _____ Fax: _____

E-mail: _____

Name: _____

Address: _____

Phone: _____ Fax: _____

E-mail: _____

Trustees for trusts set up in the will (trusts for minor children, spousal trust, etc.)

❑ Same as Executor(s)/Estate Trustee(s)

Name: _____

Address: _____

Phone: _____ Fax: _____

E-mail: _____

Name: _____

Address: _____

Phone: _____ Fax: _____

E-mail: _____

Name: _____

Address: _____

Phone: _____ Fax: _____

E-mail: _____

CHAPTER FIVE

Your Assets and Liabilities

If you become incapacitated, your representative or attorney for financial affairs will need to know where all your assets are and what your liabilities are, so they can manage them on your behalf.

On your death, your executor will need to be able to locate all of your assets and liabilities, to carry out your instructions and to act in your best interests. Even if your executor is a family member, don't assume he or she knows all the details of your financial life. There can be added expenses and unnecessary delays, not to mention the added stress on those who have to manage your finances, if they cannot find your documents and assets easily.

In this chapter, you'll find worksheets to record what you've got and what you owe. Your personal inventory, the "what" of your financial life, can help you with your own planning and help your financial advisor or planner better understand your financial situation.

YOUR ASSETS

It used to be that Canadians held most of their assets in their own name and let the will distribute their assets. Today, with concerns about probate taxes (at its maximum 1.5% and much less in some provinces), some people have set up assets in joint names and used other strategies, rather than letting the instructions in their will handle the distribution.

But I've noticed a recent trend. People who want to ensure that their estate will be distributed equitably on an after-tax basis to their children, or who want to take advantage of the potential tax savings a testamentary trust might offer, are undoing some of their joint registrations and designating their "estate" as the beneficiary on certain assets.

Only assets registered in your own name are distributed through your will (unless you own them as joint tenancy in common). But your overall financial picture consists of not just the assets that are distributed through your will, but also those assets you own jointly with rights of survivorship, as well as assets where you have designated a beneficiary.

The following worksheet provides you with an opportunity to revisit the registration of your assets—and to discuss the appropriate strategies with your professional advisor.

FINANCIAL ASSETS WORKSHEET

The purpose of this worksheet is to provide a central list of all your assets, the financial institution you deal with as well as your account numbers, so your attorney or executor can locate your assets and deal with them on your behalf.

When completing this information, don't guess. If you are not sure of the details of your account, check with your financial institution. For example, if you are not sure who is named as your beneficiary on your RRSPs, RRIFs, or company pension plan, and it is not indicated on your most recent statement, contact the financial institution or representative to find out who, if anyone, is named. If the information is out of date, you can request that it be updated.

If you have statements for any asset listed here that shows the account number and all the other information, attach a copy of it to this asset list, so your executor has quick access to all the information. Since the actual values of your accounts are constantly changing, consider attaching a copy of the year-end statement, the one dated December 31st, each year.

The legend for the registration of title of your assets in the following section is as follows:

S   Sole owner—where the asset is registered in your name only

JS   Joint tenants with rights of survivorship (JTWROS)—where two or more people are on title as owners. On the death of one owner, the deceased's interest in the asset is passed to the surviving owner(s).

JC   Joint tenants in common—where two or more people are on title as owners. On death, the deceased's owner's share is distributed according to the instructions in his or her will.

For planning purposes, record the details of your entire estate and how the ownership is registered. But remember, assets which have a named beneficiary, or are owned jointly with rights of survivorship, are not distributed according to your will.

As with all the worksheets in this workbook, not all the sections will apply to you.

Date Completed _____

Date Updated   _____

BANK ACCOUNTS

Although you may not be earning much in the way of interest on these accounts, here's the place to list your bank accounts. Don't forget about any accounts in U.S. dollars or other currencies.

Type of Account ❑ Savings ❑ Chequing ❑ Other: _____

Owner(s): _____ ❑ S ❑ JS ❑ JC

Name of institution: _____

Account number: _____

Currency ❑ C$ ❑ US$ ❑ Other: _____ Approximate balance: $ _____

Type of Account   ❑ Savings   ❑ Chequing   ❑ Other: _____

Owner(s): _____ ❑ S ❑ JS ❑ JC

Name of institution: _____

Account number: _____

Currency   ❑ C$ ❑ US$ ❑ Other: _____   Approximate balance: $ _____

Type of Account   ❑ Savings   ❑ Chequing   ❑ Other: _____

Owner(s): _____ ❑ S ❑ JS ❑ JC

Name of institution: _____

Account number: _____

Currency   ❑ C$ ❑ US$ ❑ Other: _____   Approximate balance: $ _____

Type of Account   ❑ Savings   ❑ Chequing   ❑ Other: _____

Owner(s): _____ ❑ S ❑ JS ❑ JC

Name of institution: _____

Account number: _____

Currency   ❑ C$ ❑ US$ ❑ Other: _____   Approximate balance: $ _____

Type of Account   ❑ Savings   ❑ Chequing   ❑ Other: _____

Owner(s): _____ ❑ S ❑ JS ❑ JC

Name of institution: _____

Account number: _____

Currency   ❑ C$ ❑ US$ ❑ Other: _____   Approximate balance: $ _____

Are you sure you've recorded all your bank accounts? The Public Curator of Quebec recently reported it has approximately $84 million dollars of unclaimed investments that it would like to return to its rightful owners. If you want to check Quebec's registry of unclaimed property, go to www.curateur.gouv.qc.ca/cura/html/anglais/home.html.

To check Canada's main registry for unclaimed property, visit the Bank of Canada's web site for unclaimed bank balances (at last count, there were over 770,000 unclaimed accounts) at ucbswww.bank-banque-canada.ca.

CANADA SAVINGS BONDS

List any Canada Savings Bonds that are not listed on the investment or RRSP/RRIF statements you receive. Attach a copy of the latest correspondence you have received regarding your Canada Savings Bonds or a copy of the purchase agreement for any bonds you have not yet picked up.

Owner(s): _____ ❏ S ❏ JS ❏ JC

Bondholder account no.: _____ Rate: _____

Location: _____

Series: _____ Maturity date:_____ Face amount: $ _____

Owner(s): _____ ❏ S ❏ JS ❏ JC

Bondholder account no.: _____ Rate: _____

Location: _____

Series: _____ Maturity date:_____ Face amount: $ _____

Owner(s): _____ ❏ S ❏ JS ❏ JC

Bondholder account no.: _____ Rate: _____

Location: _____

Series: _____ Maturity date:_____ Face amount: $ _____

Owner(s): _____ ❏ S ❏ JS ❏ JC

Bondholder account no.: _____ Rate: _____

Location: _____

Series: _____ Maturity date:_____ Face amount: $ _____

Owner(s): _____ ❏ S ❏ JS ❏ JC

Bondholder account no.: _____ Rate: _____

Location: _____

Series: _____ Maturity date:_____ Face amount: $ _____

PROVINCIAL SAVINGS BONDS

List any provincial Savings Bonds that are not listed on the investment or RRSP/RRIF statements you receive. Attach a copy of the latest correspondence you have received regarding your provincial Savings Bonds or the purchase agreement for any bonds you have not picked up yet.

Owner(s): _____ ❏ S ❏ JS ❏ JC

Bondholder account no.: _____ Rate: _____

Province: _____ Location: _____

Series: _____ Maturity date: _____ Face amount: $ _____

Owner(s): _____ ❏ S ❏ JS ❏ JC

Bondholder account no.: _____ Rate: _____

Province: _____ Location: _____

Series: _____ Maturity date: _____ Face amount: $ _____

GICS AND TERM DEPOSITS

List any Guaranteed Investment Certificates or Term deposits you have that do not appear on any investment or RRSP/RRIF statement you receive.

Type: ❏ Equity-linked   ❏ Compounded   ❏ Annual

Owner(s): _____ ❏ S ❏ JS ❏ JC

Name of institution: _____

Certificate no.: _____ Interest rate: _____ Maturity date: _____

Current value: $ _____

Type: ❏ Equity-linked   ❏ Compounded   ❏ Annual

Owner(s): _____ ❏ S ❏ JS ❏ JC

Name of institution: _____

Certificate no.: _____ Interest rate: _____ Maturity date: _____

Current value: $ _____

Type: ❑ Equity-linked   ❑ Compounded   ❑ Annual

Owner(s): _____   ❑ S ❑ JS ❑ JC

Name of institution: _____

Certificate no.: _____   Interest rate: _____   Maturity date: _____

Current value: $ _____

Type: ❑ Equity-linked   ❑ Compounded   ❑ Annual

Owner(s): _____   ❑ S ❑ JS ❑ JC

Name of institution: _____

Certificate no.: _____   Interest rate: _____   Maturity date: _____

Current value: $ _____

Type: ❑ Equity-linked   ❑ Compounded   ❑ Annual

Owner(s): _____   ❑ S ❑ JS ❑ JC

Name of institution: _____

Certificate no.: _____   Interest rate: _____   Maturity date: _____

Current value: $ _____

Type: ❑ Equity-linked   ❑ Compounded   ❑ Annual

Owner(s): _____   ❑ S ❑ JS ❑ JC

Name of institution: _____

Certificate no.: _____   Interest rate: _____   Maturity date: _____

Current value: $ _____

Type: ❑ Equity-linked   ❑ Compounded   ❑ Annual

Owner(s): _____   ❑ S ❑ JS ❑ JC

Name of institution: _____

Certificate no.: _____   Interest rate: _____   Maturity date: _____

Current value: $ _____

GOVERNMENT, PROVINCIAL, MORTGAGE-BACKED SECURITIES OR CORPORATE BONDS/DEBENTURES

List any of the above fixed income investments you hold in certificate form. These do not include those held in investment accounts or registered plans.

Owner(s): _____ ❑ S ❑ JS ❑ JC

Description: _____

Certificate no.: _____ Face amount: $ _____

Maturity date: _____ Market value: $ _____

Owner(s): _____ ❑ S ❑ JS ❑ JC

Description: _____

Certificate no.: _____ Face amount: $ _____

Maturity date: _____ Market value: $ _____

Owner(s): _____ ❑ S ❑ JS ❑ JC

Description: _____

Certificate no.: _____ Face amount: $ _____

Maturity date: _____ Market value: $ _____

Owner(s): _____ ❑ S ❑ JS ❑ JC

Description: _____

Certificate no.: _____ Face amount: $ _____

Maturity date: _____ Market value: $ _____

Owner(s): _____ ❑ S ❑ JS ❑ JC

Description: _____

Certificate no.: _____ Face amount: $ _____

Maturity date: _____ Market value: $ _____

STOCKS

It's time to account for any stocks you hold in certificate form. If they are not stored in your safety deposit box, make a note of where they are stored. Do not include stocks held in investment accounts or registered plans.

The ACB is the "adjusted cost base" for tax purposes. The difference between the current market value and the ACB is the profit, or the capital gain. Under the current tax rules, 50% of the capital gain is taxable when the investment is sold, or deemed to have been sold.

Owner(s): _____ ❏ S ❏ JS ❏ JC

Name of stock: _____ Stock symbol: _____

Certificate nos: _____ No. of shares: _____

ACB: _____ Market value: $ _____

Owner(s): _____ ❏ S ❏ JS ❏ JC

Name of stock: _____ Stock symbol: _____

Certificate nos: _____ No. of shares: _____

ACB: _____ Market value: $ _____

Owner(s): _____ ❏ S ❏ JS ❏ JC

Name of stock: _____ Stock symbol: _____

Certificate nos: _____ No. of shares: _____

ACB: _____ Market value: $ _____

Owner(s): _____ ❏ S ❏ JS ❏ JC

Name of stock: _____ Stock symbol: _____

Certificate nos: _____ No. of shares: _____

ACB: _____ Market value: $ _____

Owner(s): _____ ❏ S ❏ JS ❏ JC

Name of stock: _____ Stock symbol: _____

Certificate nos: _____ No. of shares: _____

ACB: _____ Market value: $ _____

Does it make sense to deposit these share certificates into an investment account with a broker, where any dividends, stock splits, and reorganizations could be handled on your behalf by your broker? This could also help settle your estate more quickly. Your executor would only have to send supporting documentation once to the brokerage firm to arrange for the account to be re-registered in the name of the estate. Otherwise, your executor will have to send the original share certificates, along with the required documentation—including a copy of the will, a copy of the death certificate, and a copy of the grant or letters or probate—to the representative or trustee of each company to have the shares re-registered in the name of the estate or transferred to the beneficiary.

STOCK OPTIONS

It has become popular to offer key employees stock options as part of their compensation package. With the "tech wreck" and recent market conditions, some stock options are not worth the paper they are printed on, but some are.

Employer: _____

Employee: _____

Date of employment: _____ No. of shares: _____

Year exercisable: _____ Exercise price: $ _____

Expiry date: _____ Deferred? ❑ Yes ❑ No   Estimated value: $ _____

Employer: _____

Employee: _____

Date of employment: _____ No. of shares: _____

Year exercisable: _____ Exercise price: $ _____

Expiry date: _____ Deferred? ❑ Yes ❑ No   Estimated value: $ _____

MUTUAL FUNDS HELD DIRECT

List any mutual fund investments you hold direct. Do not include those that are held in investment accounts or registered plans through your broker or financial planning firm, since you'll be asked about these later in this chapter.

Owner(s): _____ ❑ S ❑ JS ❑ JC

Name of fund: _____

Account no.: _____ Fund co./Institution: _____

No. of units: _____ Statement attached? ❑ Yes ❑ No

ACB: _____ Market value: $ _____

Owner(s): _____ ❑ S ❑ JS ❑ JC

Name of fund: _____

Account no.: _____ Fund co./Institution: _____

No. of units: _____ Statement attached? ❑ Yes ❑ No

ACB: _____ Market value: $ _____

Owner(s): _____ ❑ S ❑ JS ❑ JC

Name of fund: _____

Account no.: _____ Fund co./Institution: _____

No. of units: _____ Statement attached? ❑ Yes ❑ No

ACB: _____ Market value: $ _____

Owner(s): _____ ❑ S ❑ JS ❑ JC

Name of fund: _____

Account no.: _____ Fund co./Institution: _____

No. of units: _____ Statement attached? ❑ Yes ❑ No

ACB: _____ Market value: $ _____

Owner(s): _____ ❑ S ❑ JS ❑ JC

Name of fund: _____

Account no.: _____ Fund co./Institution: _____

No. of units: _____ Statement attached? ❑ Yes ❑ No

ACB: _____ Market value: $ _____

INVESTMENT ACCOUNTS

Include investment accounts at banks, trust companies, mutual fund companies, brokerage firms, financial planning or investment counselling firms, etc. that are *not* held in a RRSP, GRRSP, RRIF, or DPSP.

Owner(s): _____   ❑ S ❑ JS ❑ JC

Account no.: _____ Name of institution: _____

Statement attached? ❑ Yes ❑ No   Market value: $ _____

Owner(s): _____   ❑ S ❑ JS ❑ JC

Account no.: _____ Name of institution: _____

Statement attached? ❑ Yes ❑ No   Market value: $ _____

Owner(s): _____   ❑ S ❑ JS ❑ JC

Account no.: _____ Name of institution: _____

Statement attached? ❑ Yes ❑ No   Market value: $ _____

Owner(s): _____   ❑ S ❑ JS ❑ JC

Account no.: _____ Name of institution: _____

Statement attached? ❑ Yes ❑ No   Market value: $ _____

Owner(s): _____   ❑ S ❑ JS ❑ JC

Account no.: _____ Name of institution: _____

Statement attached? ❑ Yes ❑ No   Market value: $ _____

Is it time to simplify your financial affairs? If yes, consider consolidating some of your investment accounts.

TAX-SHELTERED INVESTMENTS

This includes investments such as oil and gas partnerships, mutual fund limited partnerships, real estate partnerships, films, and labour-sponsored funds, etc. Even though you might want to forget you ever invested in some of these tax-sheltered investments, your executor will need to know where they are.

Owner(s): _____ ❑ S ❑ JS ❑ JC

Description: _____

Partnership no.: _____ Institution: _____

Statement attached? ❑ Yes ❑ No   ACB: _____ Market value: $ _____

Owner(s): _____ ❑ S ❑ JS ❑ JC

Description: _____

Partnership no.: _____ Institution: _____

Statement attached? ❑ Yes ❑ No   ACB: _____ Market value: $ _____

Owner(s): _____ ❑ S ❑ JS ❑ JC

Description: _____

Partnership no.: _____ Institution: _____

Statement attached? ❑ Yes ❑ No   ACB: _____ Market value: $ _____

REGISTERED ACCOUNTS AND PENSION PLANS

Here's the place to list your Registered Retirement Savings Plans (RRSPs), locked-in RRSPs, where the money came from a former company pension plan, as well as any group RRSPs or company deferred pension savings plans (DPSP) you might have.

RRSP/Spousal RRSP/Locked-in RRSP/GRRSP/DPSP

Type: ❑ RRSP   ❑ Spousal RRSP   ❑ Locked-in RRSP   ❑ LIRA   ❑ GRRSP   ❑ DPSP

Annuitant: _____ Named beneficiary: _____

Account no.: _____ Institution: _____

Balance of LifeLong Learning/HomeBuyers Program: $ _____

Statement attached? ❑ Yes ❑ No   Market value: $ _____

Type: ❑ RRSP   ❑ Spousal RRSP   ❑ Locked-in RRSP   ❑ LIRA   ❑ GRRSP   ❑ DPSP

Annuitant: _____   Named beneficiary: _____

Account no.: _____   Institution: _____

Balance of LifeLong Learning/HomeBuyers Program: $ _____

Statement attached?   ❑ Yes ❑ No   Market value: $ _____

Type: ❑ RRSP   ❑ Spousal RRSP   ❑ Locked-in RRSP   ❑ LIRA   ❑ GRRSP   ❑ DPSP

Annuitant: _____   Named beneficiary: _____

Account no.: _____   Institution: _____

Balance of LifeLong Learning/HomeBuyers Program: $ _____

Statement attached?   ❑ Yes ❑ No   Market value: $ _____

Type: ❑ RRSP   ❑ Spousal RRSP   ❑ Locked-in RRSP   ❑ LIRA   ❑ GRRSP   ❑ DPSP

Annuitant: _____   Named beneficiary: _____

Account no.: _____   Institution: _____

Balance of LifeLong Learning/HomeBuyers Program: $ _____

Statement attached?   ❑ Yes ❑ No   Market value: $ _____

RRIF/LIF/LIRA

A Registered Retirement Income Fund (RRIF) generates retirement income. On death, a RRIF can be left to a named beneficiary, or to a successor annuitant who would continue to receive income from the plan.

Type: ❑ RRIF   ❑ LIF   ❑ Spousal RRIF

Annuitant: _____   Named beneficiary: _____

Account no.: _____   Institution: _____

Successor annuitant?   ❑ Yes ❑ No   Name: _____

Statement attached?   ❑ Yes ❑ No   Market value: $ _____

Type: ❑ RRIF   ❑ LIF   ❑ Spousal RRIF

Annuitant: _____   Named beneficiary: _____

Account no.: _____   Institution: _____

Successor annuitant?   ❑ Yes ❑ No   Name: _____

Statement attached?   ❑ Yes ❑ No   Market value: $ _____

Type: ❑ RRIF   ❑ LIF   ❑ Spousal RRIF

Annuitant: _____   Named beneficiary: _____

Account no.: _____   Institution: _____

Successor annuitant?   ❑ Yes ❑ No   Name: _____

Statement attached?   ❑ Yes ❑ No   Market value: $ _____

Type: ❑ RRIF   ❑ LIF   ❑ Spousal RRIF

Annuitant: _____   Named beneficiary: _____

Account no.: _____   Institution: _____

Successor annuitant?   ❑ Yes ❑ No   Name: _____

Statement attached?   ❑ Yes ❑ No   Market value: $ _____

EMPLOYER PENSION PLANS

The retirement income from a defined benefit plan (DBP) is based on a formula that is normally based on the employee's years of service and income. The retirement income from a defined contribution plan (DCP) is based on the value of the contributions and earnings at the time of retirement.

Pension plans may have one method of determining the death benefit for those dying before retirement, and another method for determining the death benefit (such as a survivor pension), if death occurs in retirement.

Don't forget to include any pension benefits you may still have with a former employer—one where you left your pension entitlement with them rather than transferring it to a locked-in RRSP!

Type: ❑ Defined Benefit Plan (DBP)   ❑ Defined Contribution Plan (DCP)   ❑ Other: _____

Employee: _____   Beneficiary: _____

Employer: _____   Policy/Certificate no.: _____

Annual income at retirement: $ _____   Indexed?   ❑ Yes   ❑ No

Death benefit: Before retirement: _____   In retirement: _____

❑ Current employer   ❑ Former employer   ❑ Retired

Type: ❑ Defined Benefit Plan (DBP)   ❑ Defined Contribution Plan (DCP)   ❑ Other: _____

Employee: _____   Beneficiary: _____

Employer: _____   Policy/Certificate no.: _____

Annual income at retirement: $ _____   Indexed?   ❑ Yes   ❑ No

Death benefit: Before retirement: _____   In retirement: _____

❑ Current employer   ❑ Former employer   ❑ Retired

Type: ❑ Defined Benefit Plan (DBP)   ❑ Defined Contribution Plan (DCP)   ❑ Other: _____

Employee: _____   Beneficiary: _____

Employer: _____   Policy/Certificate no.: _____

Annual income at retirement: $ _____   Indexed?   ❑ Yes   ❑ No

Death benefit: Before retirement: _____   In retirement: _____

❑ Current employer   ❑ Former employer   ❑ Retired

RCA/SERP/OTHER

Some entrepreneurs and senior executives may have other deferred forms of retirement compensation such as a retirement compensation agreement (RCA) or a supplemental Executive Retirement Program (SERP), or an Individual Pension Plan (IPP).

Type: ❏ Retirement Compensation Agreement (RCA)   ❏ Individual Pension Plan (IPP)

   ❏ Supplemental Executive Retirement Program (SERP)   ❏ Other: _____

Annuitant: _____   Named beneficiary: _____

Plan: _____   Institution: _____

Description: _____

Statement attached? ❏ Yes ❏ No   Market value: $ _____

OTHER ASSETS

Gold/Silver/Other

Owner(s): _____ ❏ S ❏ JS ❏ JC

Description: _____

Location: _____ Market value: $ _____

Owner(s): _____ ❏ S ❏ JS ❏ JC

Description: _____

Location: _____ Market value: $ _____

RESPs

Have you set up a registered education savings program for children or grandchildren?

Subscriber(s): _____ ❏ Family   ❏ Individual

Beneficiaries: _____

Account no.: _____ Fund co./Institution: _____

Year established: _____   Statement attached? ❏ Yes ❏ No   Market value: $ _____

Subscriber(s): _____ ❏ Family   ❏ Individual

Beneficiaries: _____

Account no.: _____ Fund co./Institution: _____

Year established: _____   Statement attached? ❏ Yes ❏ No   Market value: $ _____

In-Trust for Accounts

Do you have any informal trust account(s) for which you are the trustee for a minor child or grandchild?

Beneficiary: _____

Trustee(s): _____

Account no.:_____ Fund co./Institution: _____

Statement attached? ❏ Yes ❏ No   Market value: $ _____

Beneficiary: _____

Trustee(s): _____

Account no.:_____ Fund co./Institution: _____

Statement attached? ❏ Yes ❏ No   Market value: $ _____

Beneficiary: _____

Trustee(s): _____

Account no.:_____ Fund co./Institution: _____

Statement attached? ❏ Yes ❏ No   Market value: $ _____

U.S. Situs Assets

Do you own any assets that are located in the U.S., such as real estate, a U.S. investment account, etc.?

Owner(s): _____ ❏ S ❏ JS ❏ JC

Description: _____

Account no.:_____ Institution: _____

Statement attached? ❏ Yes ❏ No   Market value: $ _____

Owner(s): _____ ❏ S ❏ JS ❏ JC

Description: _____

Account no.:_____ Institution: _____

Statement attached? ❏ Yes ❏ No   Market value: $ _____

Other Assets Outside of Canada and the U.S.

Do you own assets outside of Canada and the U.S.? Don't forget about them.

Owner(s): _____ ❏ S ❏ JS ❏ JC

Description: _____

Account no.:_____ Institution: _____

Statement attached? ❏ Yes ❏ No Market value: $ _____

Owner(s): _____ ❏ S ❏ JS ❏ JC

Description: _____

Account no.:_____ Institution: _____

Statement attached? ❏ Yes ❏ No Market value: $ _____

Holding Company

Do you have an incorporated company that now functions as a holding company for your investment portfolio?

Shareholder(s): _____

Percentage interest: _____ Assets: _____

Statement attached? ❏ Yes ❏ No Value of interest: $ _____

Living Trust(s)/Alter Ego Trust

Name of estate/trust: _____

Settlor: _____ Trustee: _____

Beneficiaries: _____

Description of interest: _____ Percentage interest: _____

End Date: _____ Value of interest: $ _____

Name of estate/trust: _____

Settlor: _____ Trustee: _____

Beneficiaries: _____

Description of interest: _____ Percentage interest: _____

End Date: _____ Value of interest: $ _____

Antiques, Artwork, Jewelry, Special Collections

List each item valued at more than $1,000 separately. Attach a separate list if required.

Owner(s): _____ ❏ S ❏ JS ❏ JC

Description: _____

Location: _____

Date purchased: _____ Appraised value: $_____

Owner(s): _____ ❏ S ❏ JS ❏ JC

Description: _____

Location: _____

Date purchased: _____ Appraised value: $_____

Owner(s): _____ ❏ S ❏ JS ❏ JC

Description: _____

Location: _____

Date purchased: _____ Appraised value: $_____

Owner(s): _____ ❏ S ❏ JS ❏ JC

Description: _____

Location: _____

Date purchased: _____ Appraised value: $_____

Owner(s): _____ ❏ S ❏ JS ❏ JC

Description: _____

Location: _____

Date purchased: _____ Appraised value: $_____

Owner(s): _____ ❏ S ❏ JS ❏ JC

Description: _____

Location: _____

Date purchased: _____ Appraised value: $_____

Cars, Vans, Trucks, Boats, Planes

Include the vehicles parked in your driveway as well as those parked elsewhere.

Registered owner(s): _____ ❑ S ❑ JS ❑ JC

Description: _____ Serial No.: _____

Make/Model: _____ Year: _____

Location of maintenance records: _____ Licence no. _____

❑ Leased? Details of lease: _____

❑ Purchased? Date purchased: _____ Cost: _____

Market Value: $_____

Registered owner(s): _____ ❑ S ❑ JS ❑ JC

Description: _____ Serial No.: _____

Make/Model: _____ Year: _____

Location of maintenance records: _____ Licence no. _____

❑ Leased? Details of lease: _____

❑ Purchased? Date purchased: _____ Cost: _____

Market Value: $_____

Registered owner(s): _____ ❑ S ❑ JS ❑ JC

Description: _____ Serial No.: _____

Make/Model: _____ Year: _____

Location of maintenance records: _____ Licence no. _____

❑ Leased? Details of lease: _____

❑ Purchased? Date purchased: _____ Cost: _____

Market Value: $_____

Private Loans/Mortgage Held (including family promissory notes to be paid to you)

Name of borrower: _____ Relationship: _____

Loan made by: _____

Terms of loan: _____

Written loan agreement? ❑ Yes ❑ No   Agreement attached? ❑ Yes ❑ No

To be forgiven at death? ❑ Yes ❑ No   Outstanding balance: $ _____

Name of borrower: _____ Relationship: _____

Loan made by: _____

Terms of loan: _____

Written loan agreement? ❑ Yes ❑ No   Agreement attached? ❑ Yes ❑ No

To be forgiven at death? ❑ Yes ❑ No   Outstanding balance: $ _____

Name of borrower: _____ Relationship: _____

Loan made by: _____

Terms of loan: _____

Written loan agreement? ❑ Yes ❑ No   Agreement attached? ❑ Yes ❑ No

To be forgiven at death? ❑ Yes ❑ No   Outstanding balance: $ _____

Safety Deposit Box

Institution: _____

Address: _____

Box no.: _____ Where is the key? _____

Who has signing authority? _____ Contents (List attached) ❑ Yes ❑ No

Institution: _____

Address: _____

Box no.: _____ Where is the key? _____

Who has signing authority? _____ Contents (List attached) ❑ Yes ❑ No

Other Safe-Keeping/Storage

Do you have any items held in mini-storage, a personal safe, personal mail box, gym locker, etc.?

Description: _____

Location: _____

Location of keys: _____ Contents (List attached): ❏ Yes ❏ No

Description: _____

Location: _____

Location of keys: _____ Contents (List attached): ❏ Yes ❏ No

Intellectual Property Rights

Are you an artist, writer, inventor or do you otherwise hold any intellectual property rights?

❏ Copyright   ❏ Patent   ❏ Trademarks   ❏ Licence   ❏ Other: _____

Description: _____

❏ Copyright   ❏ Patent   ❏ Trademarks   ❏ Licence   ❏ Other: _____

Description: _____

Do you receive payments or are you entitled to receive payments from:

Yes No
❏ ❏ CanCopy

❏ ❏ Other:_____

❏ ❏ Other:_____

REAL ESTATE WORKSHEET

This worksheet is for home, sweet home—and all the other property you have the pleasure of owning.

Date Completed _____

Date Updated _____

Principal Residence

Owner(s): _____ ❏ S ❏ JS ❏ JC

Address: _____

Description: _____ Location of deed: _____

Purchase price: _____ Date purchased: _____

Matrimonial home? ❏ Yes ❏ No   Estimated market value: $ _____

Vacation Properties (cottage/timeshare/cabin/camp/etc.)

Owner(s): _____ ❏ S ❏ JS ❏ JC

Address: _____

Description: _____ Location of deed: _____

Purchase price: _____ Date purchased: _____

Matrimonial home? ❏ Yes ❏ No   Estimated market value: $ _____

Investment Properties

Owner(s): _____ ❏ S ❏ JS ❏ JC

Address: _____

Description: _____ Location of deed: _____

Purchase price: _____ Date purchased: _____

Is the property currently leased? ❏ Yes ❏ No   Location of lease: _____

Date lease renews: _____ Estimated market value: $ _____

Vacant Land

Owner(s): _____ ❏ S ❏ JS ❏ JC

Address: _____

Description: _____ Location of deed: _____

Purchase price: _____ Date Purchased: _____

Estimated market value: $ _____

GENERAL AND HEALTH INSURANCE WORKSHEET

Use this worksheet to list your general and health insurance so your executor can collect any death benefits payable, or if you become mentally incapable, your attorney or representative can claim any critical illness or medical benefits you are entitled to. You will also want your executor to handle any house or car insurance policies you have, so you don't pay premiums for longer than necessary.

Date Completed _____

Date Updated _____

Auto/Vehicle Insurance Policies

Vehicle description: _____

Company: _____ Policy no.: _____

Policy owner(s): _____

Description of insurance: _____

Location of policy: _____ Policy expiry date: _____

Vehicle description: _____

Company: _____ Policy no.: _____

Policy owner(s): _____

Description of insurance: _____

Location of policy: _____ Policy expiry date: _____

Property Insurance Policies

Description of insured property: _____

Company: _____ Policy no.: _____

Policy owner(s): _____ Location of policy: _____

Replacement coverage? ❑ Yes ❑ No   Policy expiry date: _____

Description of insured property: _____

Company: _____ Policy no.: _____

Policy owner(s): _____ Location of policy: _____

Replacement coverage? ❏ Yes ❏ No   Policy expiry date: _____

Health and Medical Coverage

In addition to your provincial coverage and the coverage you may have through a current or former employer (if retired), do you have any extended medical or health insurance (such as coverage for while outside Canada, or coverage through a private insurer)?

Company: _____ Policy no.: _____

Type of coverage: _____ People covered: _____

Location of policy: _____ Policy expiry date: _____

Company: _____ Policy no.: _____

Type of coverage: _____ People covered: _____

Location of policy: _____ Policy expiry date: _____

Critical Illness or Long-Term Care Coverage

While insurance policies that cover critical illness and long-term care are relatively new in Canada, you will want your power of attorney, mandate, or representative to know if there may be money to help with the bills.

Type: ❏ Critical Illness ❏ Long-Term Care ❏ Other:_____

Policy owner(s): _____ Beneficiary: _____

Lives insured: _____

Company: _____ Policy no.: _____

     Death benefit: $_____

Type: ❏ Critical Illness ❏ Long-Term Care ❏ Other:_____

Policy owner(s): _____ Beneficiary: _____

Lives insured: _____

Company: _____ Policy no.: _____

     Death benefit: $_____

LIFE INSURANCE WORKSHEET (INDIVIDUAL, GROUP, AND ASSOCIATION)

What good is having life insurance if your executor or the beneficiary does not know it exists?

Use this worksheet to list all life insurance coverage you have, including individual life insurance policies, group life insurance, and any life insurance you may have through your professional association, credit cards and clubs, such as the Canadian Automobile Association (CAA).

You'll also find room to list any disability, and accidental death and dismemberment insurance you may have.

Date Completed   _____

Date Updated   _____

Type: ❑ Term   ❑ Term-100   ❑ Universal Life   ❑ Group Life

        ❑ Endowment   ❑ Joint 1st to die   ❑ Joint 2nd to die   ❑ Other: _____

Policy owner(s): _____   Beneficiary: _____

Lives insured: _____   Purpose: _____

Company: _____   Policy no.: _____

Policy expiry date: _____   Loan balance: _____

Current cash value: $ _____   Death benefit: $ _____

Type: ❑ Term   ❑ Term-100   ❑ Universal Life   ❑ Group Life

        ❑ Endowment   ❑ Joint 1st to die   ❑ Joint 2nd to die   ❑ Other: _____

Policy owner(s): _____   Beneficiary: _____

Lives insured: _____   Purpose: _____

Company: _____   Policy no.: _____

Policy expiry date: _____   Loan balance: _____

Current cash value: $ _____   Death benefit: $ _____

Type: ❑ Term   ❑ Term-100   ❑ Universal Life   ❑ Group Life

      ❑ Endowment   ❑ Joint 1st to die   ❑ Joint 2nd to die   ❑ Other:_____

Policy owner(s): _____   Beneficiary: _____

Lives insured: _____   Purpose: _____

Company: _____   Policy no.: _____

Policy expiry date: _____   Loan balance: _____

Current cash value: $ _____   Death benefit: $ _____

Type: ❑ Term   ❑ Term-100   ❑ Universal Life   ❑ Group Life

      ❑ Endowment   ❑ Joint 1st to die   ❑ Joint 2nd to die   ❑ Other:_____

Policy owner(s): _____   Beneficiary: _____

Lives insured: _____   Purpose: _____

Company: _____   Policy no.: _____

Policy expiry date: _____   Loan balance: _____

Current cash value: $ _____   Death benefit: $ _____

Disability and Accidental Death and Dismemberment Coverage

You may have disability insurance through your employer, or if you are self-employed or a professional, you may have disability insurance you have purchased.

You may have a separate policy for accidental death and dismemberment (AD&D)—you may even have $1,000 or $5,000 of free coverage that was sent to you by a financial institution—for a limited period of time.

Type: ❑ Disability   ❑ AD&D   ❑ Other:_____

Policy owner(s): _____   Beneficiary: _____

Lives insured: _____

Company: _____   Policy no.: _____

                                 Death benefit: $_____

Type: ❑ Disability   ❑ AD&D   ❑ Other:_____

Policy owner(s): _____   Beneficiary: _____

Lives insured: _____

Company: _____   Policy no.: _____

Death benefit: $_____

Segregated Funds

Policy owner(s): _____   Beneficiary: _____

Lives insured: _____

Company: _____   Policy no.: _____

Last reset date: _____   Statement attached? ❑ Yes ❑ No

Guarantee value: $ _____   Current market value: $_____

Policy owner(s): _____   Beneficiary: _____

Lives insured: _____

Company: _____   Policy no.: _____

Last reset date: _____   Statement attached? ❑ Yes ❑ No

Guarantee value: $ _____   Current market value: $_____

Policy owner(s): _____   Beneficiary: _____

Lives insured: _____

Company: _____   Policy no.: _____

Last reset date: _____   Statement attached? ❑ Yes ❑ No

Guarantee value: $ _____   Current market value: $_____

Annuities

Type: ❑ Registered ❑ Regular ❑ Prescribed ❑ Charitable ❑ Other: _____

Annuitant(s): _____ Beneficiary: _____

Company: _____ Policy no.: _____

Issue date: _____ Guaranteed period: _____

Guarantee expiry date: _____ Annual income: $ _____

Type: ❑ Registered ❑ Regular ❑ Prescribed ❑ Charitable ❑ Other: _____

Annuitant(s): _____ Beneficiary: _____

Company: _____ Policy no: _____

Issue date: _____ Guaranteed period: _____

Guarantee expiry date: _____ Annual income: $ _____

Other Assets

Do you own anything else?

Owner(s): _____ ❑ S ❑ JS ❑ JC

Description: _____ Serial no.: _____

Model: _____ Year: _____

Date purchased: _____ Cost: $ _____ Market value: $ _____

Owner(s): _____ ❑ S ❑ JS ❑ JC

Description: _____ Serial no.: _____

Model: _____ Year: _____

Date purchased: _____ Cost: $ _____ Market value: $ _____

BUSINESS AND OTHER ENTREPRENEURIAL INTERESTS WORKSHEET

If you own a business or farm, you have to consider these assets as part of your estate planning, as well as your succession plan.

Date Completed _____

Date Updated _____

Business name: _____

Business address: _____

City/Province/Postal code: _____

Phone no.: _____ Fax no.: _____

E-mail: _____

Type: ❑ Sole proprietorship ❑ Partnership ❑ Corporation ❑ Farm ❑ Other: _____

Nature of business: _____

Name of bookkeeper: _____ Phone no.: _____

Market value: $_____

Business Identification Number (BIN): _____

Goods and Services (GST) or Harmonized Sales Tax (HST) Number:_____

BUSINESS BANK ACCOUNT

Name of institution: _____

Account no.: _____ Approximate balance: $ _____

BUSINESS INVESTMENT PORTFOLIO

Registered owner: _____

Account no.: _____ Name of institution: _____

Statement attached? ❑ Yes ❑ No Market value: $_____

Registered owner: _____

Account no.: _____ Name of institution: _____

Statement attached? ❑ Yes ❑ No   Market value: $_____

BUSINESS CREDIT CARD

Description: _____ Amount owing:_____

Account no.: _____ Store or firm: _____

Balance insured? ❑ Yes ❑ No   Paid off each month? ❑ Yes ❑ No

BUSINESS LINE OF CREDIT

Description: _____ Amount owing:_____

Account no.: _____ Institution: _____

Balance insured? ❑ Yes ❑ No   Secured? ❑ Yes ❑ No

SUCCESSION PLANNING

Is there a succession plan? ❑ Yes ❑ No

If yes, describe the succession plan _____

_____

_____

_____

If a Sole Proprietorship

Location of records _____

If a Partnership:

Percentage interest held:_____ Number of partners: _____

Partnership agreement? ❑ No ❑ Yes, attach details   Date reviewed: _____

Buy/sell agreement? ❑ No ❑ Yes, attach details   Date reviewed: _____

Name of key employees/partners? _____

_____

Valuation method for partnership: _____

If Incorporated:

❑ Private   ❑ Public   Date incorporated: _____

Describe the ownership of the business: _____

Key employees/shareholders? _____

Shareholders agreement? ❑ No ❑ Yes, attach details   Date reviewed: _____

Are there restrictions on the transfer of shares? ❑ No ❑ Yes

Buy/sell agreement (attach details) ❑ No ❑ Yes

If yes, how is the buy/sell to be funded? _____

Valuation method for privately held shares: _____

No. of common shares held: _____ No. of preferred shares held: _____

Names of Major Shareholders	Percentage Interest held	Shares Held In Trust	Common or Voting?	Class of Shares	Officer?
_____	_____%	_____	_____	_____	_____
_____	_____%	_____	_____	_____	_____
_____	_____%	_____	_____	_____	_____
_____	_____%	_____	_____	_____	_____
_____	_____%	_____	_____	_____	_____

Has an estate freeze been implemented? ❑ No ❑ Yes   If yes, in what year? _____

Does the business qualify for the $500,000 small business capital gains exemption? ❑ Yes ❑ No

Has any amount already been crystallized? ❑ Yes ❑ No

If yes, please indicate in whose name:

Family member: _____ Amount: $_____

Family member: _____ Amount: $_____

Corporately-held Life Insurance

Type: ❏ Term ❏ Term-100 ❏ Universal Life ❏ Group Life

❏ Endowment ❏ Joint 1st to die ❏ Joint 2nd to die ❏ Other:_____

Policy owner: _____ Beneficiary: _____

Lives insured: _____

Company: _____ Policy no.: _____

Policy expiry date: _____ Benefit option: _____

Policy loan balance: _____ Current cash value: _____ Death benefit: $ _____

If You Own a Farm

Livestock

Description	Head Count	Value
_____	_____	_____
_____	_____	_____
_____	_____	_____

Crops

Description	Acres/Tonnage	Value
_____	_____	_____
_____	_____	_____
_____	_____	_____

Land and Buildings

Description	Year Acquired	Ownership	ACB	Market Value
_____	_____	_____	_____	_____
_____	_____	_____	_____	_____
_____	_____	_____	_____	_____

Farm Equipment

Description	ACB	Market Value
_____	_____	_____
_____	_____	_____
_____	_____	_____

Quotas

Description	Market Value
_____	_____
_____	_____

Succession Plan

Who will inherit the farm?

Name: _____ Relationship:_____ When?_____

YOUR LIABILITIES

The value of your estate is settled according to the instructions in your will and consists of all the assets registered in your own name, less your debts, less your tax bill, and any other fees and costs your estate is required to pay.

Your executor is responsible for settling your debts. You can't just leave them behind. Your liabilities don't die with you, unless you die bankrupt.

The amount you owe will change over time. But by listing what you owe, and to whom, your executor will be able make sure your legitimate debts are settled.

FINANCIAL LIABILITIES WORKSHEET

The purpose of this worksheet is to provide a central list of all your liabilities, so your attorney, representative or executor can deal with them on your behalf.

Date Completed   _____

Date Updated   _____

Credit Cards

Description: _____ Amount owing: $ _____

Name of cardholder(s): _____

Account no.: _____ Store or firm: _____

Balance insured? ❑ Yes ❑ No   Paid off each month? ❑ Yes ❑ No

Description: _____ Amount owing: $ _____

Name of cardholder(s): _____

Account no.: _____ Store or firm: _____

Balance insured? ❑ Yes ❑ No   Paid off each month? ❑ Yes ❑ No

Description: _____ Amount owing: $ _____

Name of cardholder(s): _____

Account no.: _____ Store or firm: _____

Balance insured? ❑ Yes ❑ No   Paid off each month? ❑ Yes ❑ No

Description: _____ Amount owing: $ _____

Name of cardholder(s): _____

Account no.: _____ Store or firm: _____

Balance insured? ❑ Yes ❑ No   Paid off each month? ❑ Yes ❑ No

Description: _____ Amount owing: $ _____

Name of cardholder(s): _____

Account no.: _____ Store or firm: _____

Balance insured? ❑ Yes ❑ No   Paid off each month? ❑ Yes ❑ No

Description: _____ Amount owing: $ _____

Name of cardholder(s): _____

Account no.: _____ Store or firm: _____

Balance insured? ❑ Yes ❑ No   Paid off each month? ❑ Yes ❑ No

Lines of Credit

Description: _____ Amount owing: $ _____

Account no.: _____ Institution: _____

Balance insured? ❑ Yes ❑ No   Secured? ❑ Yes ❑ No

Description: _____ Amount owing: $ _____

Account no.: _____ Institution: _____

Balance insured? ❑ Yes ❑ No   Secured? ❑ Yes ❑ No

Description: _____ Amount owing: $ _____

Account no.:_____ Institution: _____

Balance insured? ❑ Yes ❑ No   Secured? ❑ Yes ❑ No

Car Loan

Make: _____ Model: _____ Year _____ Amount owing: $ _____

Account no.: _____ Firm or institution:_____

Balance insured? ❑ Yes ❑ No   End date:_____

Make: _____ Model: _____ Year _____ Amount owing: $ _____

Account no.:_____ Firm or institution:_____

Balance insured? ❏ Yes ❏ No   End date:_____

Student Loan

Description: _____ Amount owing: $ _____

Name of student: _____

Account no.: _____ Firm or institution: _____

Balance insured? ❏ Yes ❏ No   End date: _____

Promissory Notes/Personal Guarantees

Description: _____ Amount owing: $ _____

For whom: _____

Balance insured? ❏ Yes ❏ No   End date: _____

Description: _____ Amount owing: $ _____

For whom: _____

Balance insured? ❏ Yes ❏ No   End date: _____

Margin Accounts

Description: _____ Amount owing: $ _____

Account no.: _____ Fund co./Institution: _____

Description: _____ Amount owing: $ _____

Account no.: _____ Fund co./Institution: _____

Mortgages

❑ First Mortgage   ❑ Second Mortgage

Property: _____   Outstanding principal: _____

Details of mortgage: _____

Renewal date: _____   Balance insured?   ❑ Yes   ❑ No

Payment amount: _____   Payment dates: _____

Account no.: _____   Institution: _____

❑ First Mortgage   ❑ Second Mortgage

Property: _____   Outstanding principal: _____

Details of mortgage: _____

Renewal date: _____   Balance insured?   ❑ Yes   ❑ No

Payment amount: _____   Payment dates: _____

Account no.: _____   Institution: _____

Reverse Mortgage

Property: _____

Outstanding principal: _____

Details of mortgage: _____

Renewal date: _____

Unpaid Personal Income Taxes

Year	Amount
_____	_____
_____	_____
_____	_____

Other Debts/Liabilities

Description: _____

Amount owing: $ _____ Balance insured? ❑ Yes ❑ No

Description: _____

Amount owing: $ _____ Balance insured? ❑ Yes ❑ No

Description: _____

Amount owing: $ _____ Balance insured? ❑ Yes ❑ No

Other Financial Obligations

Certain other financial obligations could continue, even after death. For example, some separation and divorce agreements require that support be paid based on the needs of the recipient, not whether the payer is dead or alive. While these support obligations are often related to the needs of your children and spouse, some individuals have chosen to purchase life insurance to create the needed income, for as long as it is required, rather than have their estate eroded by the ongoing financial obligation.

Payments Required Under Separation or Divorce Agreement

To: _____ Relationship: _____

Obligation insured? ❑ Yes ❑ No   Annual amount: $ _____

To: _____ Relationship: _____

Obligation insured? ❑ Yes ❑ No   Annual amount: $ _____

Other Payments Required By Court Order or Other Agreement

Reason: _____ Annual amount: $ _____

Reason: _____ Annual amount: $ _____

So Who Really Gets What?

Because some of your estate may be distributed through your will, some may be distributed to a named beneficiary, and some may be owned jointly with rights of survivorship, it's often difficult to determine the end result of your estate plan—who gets what.

Some people have set up what they think will result in an even distribution, only to discover that the tax rules can disrupt the plan. It's not the total value of your assets that you have to consider, but the after-tax, after-fees, after debts-are-paid value of your estate. For example, if you name a financially independent adult child as the beneficiary of your RRSP and another financially independent adult child as the primary beneficiary of the residue of your estate, that second child could receive a smaller inheritance then you had anticipated—the value of the estate after all the taxes have been paid, including the tax due on that RRSP!

Working this through is important if you want to be sure your estate will be distributed as you wish. These worksheets are designed to help you determine who will actually get what. But remember, these worksheets will only provide you with a rough estimate of the ultimate distribution of your overall estate, since the value of your assets will increase and decrease over time and taxes and other costs of dying will change.

After you have determined the benefit to each of your beneficiaries under the various distribution methods, you can reflect on whether or not your estate will be distributed as you hope. If not, you'll need to update your estate plan. Remember, these pages are worksheets to help you plan the distribution of your estate. To distribute your estate, your will has to be properly prepared, your beneficiary designations up to date, and your registration of ownership appropriate for your situation.

ASSETS DISTRIBUTED TO DESIGNATED BENEFICIARY

List all your assets for which you have designated a named beneficiary, such as your registered retirement savings plan (RRSP), registered retirement income fund (RRIF), employer pension plan, segregated funds, and life insurance policies. Then, add up the appropriate value each designated beneficiary would receive, based on today's market values. If you find that any designation is not up-to-date, update them now.

Where an asset has more than one designated beneficiary, indicate the approximate value of his or her share of the asset.

Date Completed   _____

Date Updated   _____

TO SPOUSE/COMMON-LAW PARTNER

Name of beneficiary: _____

Assets by Type	Approximate Value
RRSP/RRIF	$_____
Life insurance	$_____
Company pension plan	$_____
Segregated funds	$_____
_____	$_____
Subtotal:	$_____

TO OTHER BENEFICIARIES

Name of beneficiary: _____

Assets by Type	Approximate Value
RRSP/RRIF	$_____
Life insurance	$_____
Company pension plan	$_____
Segregated funds	$_____
_____	$_____
Subtotal:	$_____

Name of beneficiary: _____

Assets by Type	Approximate Value
RRSP/RRIF	$_____
Life insurance	$_____
Company pension plan	$_____
Segregated funds	$_____
_____	$_____
Subtotal:	$_____

Name of beneficiary: _____

Assets by Type	Approximate Value
RRSP/RRIF	$_____
Life insurance	$_____
Company pension plan	$_____
Segregated funds	$_____
_____	$_____
Subtotal:	$_____

Name of beneficiary: _____

Assets by Type	Approximate Value
RRSP/RRIF	$_____
Life insurance	$_____
Company pension plan	$_____
Segregated funds	$_____
_____	$_____
Subtotal:	$_____

Name of beneficiary: _____

Assets by Type	Approximate Value
RRSP/RRIF	$_____
Life insurance	$_____
Company pension plan	$_____
Segregated funds	$_____
_____	$_____
Subtotal:	$_____

Name of beneficiary: _____

Assets by Type	Approximate Value
RRSP/RRIF	$_____
Life insurance	$_____
Company pension plan	$_____
Segregated funds	$_____
_____	$_____
Subtotal:	$_____

Name of beneficiary: _____

Assets by Type	Approximate Value
RRSP/RRIF	$_____
Life insurance	$_____
Company pension plan	$_____
Segregated funds	$_____
_____	$_____
Subtotal:	$_____

ASSETS OWNED JOINT TENANTS WITH RIGHTS OF SURVIVORSHIP (JTWROS)

When you own assets jointly with rights of survivorship (not available in Quebec), your share of the asset will pass to the other owners, without flowing through your will.

In this worksheet, record all the assets you own jointly with rights of survivorship and then total the value of the assets the other owners would receive on your death, based on today's market values. Where an asset has two or more owners, indicate the approximate value of his or her share.

Date Completed _____

Date Updated _____

TO SPOUSE/COMMON-LAW PARTNER

Name	Assets	Approximate Value
_____	_____	$_____
_____	_____	$_____
_____	_____	$_____

TO OTHERS

Name	Assets	Approximate Value
_____	_____	$_____
_____	_____	$_____
_____	_____	$_____
_____	_____	$_____

SUMMARY OF VALUE OF ASSETS OWNED JTWROS

Other Owners on Title	Approximate Value
Spouse/Partner	$_____
_____	$_____
_____	$_____
_____	$_____
_____	$_____
_____	$_____

GIFTS ALREADY GIVEN

You may have already started to distribute some of the assets of your estate. While some people make gifts that are really an advance on the beneficiary's inheritance, other gifts are made that are over and above any inheritance an individual might otherwise receive.

On this worksheet, record the value of all gifts that have been made that are really an advance on the value of the inheritance that individual will ultimately receive. Also indicate the gifts you plan to make within the next twelve months, if any.

Date Completed _____

Date Updated _____

TO SPOUSE/COMMON-LAW PARTNER

Name	Description of Gift	Value of Gift
_____	_____	$_____
_____	_____	$_____
_____	_____	$_____

TO OTHERS

Name	Description of Gift	Value of Gift
_____	_____	$_____
_____	_____	$_____
_____	_____	$_____
_____	_____	$_____

SUMMARY OF VALUE OF GIFTS ALREADY GIVEN, BY BENEFICIARY

Beneficiary	Approximate Value
Spouse/Partner	$_____
_____	$_____
_____	$_____
_____	$_____
_____	$_____
_____	$_____

RECEIVED/TO BE RECEIVED UNDER ANY LIVING TRUSTS

You may have transferred some of your assets to a living trust, an alter ego trust or a joint spousal trust, that will ultimately be distributed to some of your beneficiaries. This could include the shares of a private corporation held in trust.

On this worksheet, record the value of all inheritances that will ultimately be made under the trust document of a living trust. Do not include any inheritances that will be received through a testamentary trust set up in your will on this worksheet.

Date Completed _____

Date Updated _____

TO SPOUSE/COMMON-LAW PARTNER

Name	Description of Interest in the Trust	Value of Trust Interest
_____	_____	$_____
_____	_____	$_____
_____	_____	$_____

TO OTHERS

Name	Description of Interest in the Trust	Value of Trust Interest
_____	_____	$_____
_____	_____	$_____
_____	_____	$_____
_____	_____	$_____

SUMMARY OF THE VALUE OF BENEFITS RECEIVED, OR TO BE RECEIVED, UNDER A LIVING TRUST

Beneficiary	Approximate Value
Spouse/Partner	$_____
_____	$_____
_____	$_____
_____	$_____
_____	$_____
_____	$_____

INHERITANCES TO BE DISTRIBUTED THROUGH YOUR WILL

For all assets that will be distributed according to the instructions in your will, estimate the value each beneficiary named in the will would receive, based on today's market values.

To estimate the value of the residue of your estate use the next worksheet (starting on page 135).

Date Completed   _____

Date Updated   _____

TO SPOUSE/COMMON-LAW PARTNER

Name	Type	Approximate Value
_____	Bequest _____	$ _____
_____	Cash gift _____	$ _____
_____	Residue _____ %	$ _____
_____	_____	$ _____
	Total to Spouse/Partner	$ _____

TO OTHER BENEFICIARIES

Name	Type	Approximate Value
_____	Bequest _____	$ _____
_____	Bequest _____	$ _____
_____	Bequest _____	$ _____
_____	Cash gift _____	$ _____
_____	Cash gift _____	$ _____
_____	Cash gift _____	$ _____
_____	Residue _____ %	$ _____
_____	Residue _____ %	$ _____
_____	Residue _____ %	$ _____
_____	Residue _____ %	$ _____
_____	Residue _____ %	$ _____
_____	_____	$ _____
_____	_____	$ _____

ESTIMATING THE VALUE OF THE RESIDUE OF YOUR ESTATE

The value of the residue of your estate starts with the value of the assets that are registered in your own name, less your liabilities including your final income taxes, less the value of any special bequests or gifts you have indicated in your will, less other costs associated with dying.

The value of your residue may be small if most of your assets are held jointly, or if they have a designated beneficiary. On the other hand, some people today have much larger estate residues, because they want to be as equitable as possible, on an after-tax basis.

If you've already completed the Assets and Liabilities worksheets in Chapter 5, the next step is to add up the value of your assets registered in your own name and the value of your liabilities, to come up with a preliminary net worth.

Total Assets	–	Total Liabilities	= Net Worth
$_____	–	$_____	= $_____

But this amount is not the value of the residue of your estate that might be available for distribution. There are other liabilities that will have to be settled at death, including your final taxes, any probate fees or taxes, and other costs associated with dying that are generally paid out of your estate before your estate residue can be distributed. As well, any special bequests or gifts you have requested be made in your will are paid before your estate residue is distributed.

The worksheets in this chapter will help you to estimate the cost of dying and approximate the value of the residue of your estate. These worksheets are designed primarily to provide you with an idea of how the value of the residue is calculated. You'll find more information in *You Can't Take It With You: The Common-Sense Guide to Estate Planning*.

Making the Most of These Worksheets

The following worksheets, Estimating the Value of the Residue of your Estate and Estimating Your Probate Fees or Taxes, along with Estimating Your Final Tax Bill (see the following chapter), will help you estimate the residue of your estate as if you died today.

If you have a spouse or common-law partner, you can use these worksheets to estimate the residue of your estate as if you had died and were survived by your spouse or partner. Or you can use these worksheets to estimate the residue of your estate as if your spouse or partner had predeceased you. If your spouse or partner predeceases you, you are not able to defer any tax—all income taxes will have to be settled before your estate is distributed to the next generation or other family members, friends, or charity.

These worksheets will give you only a rough estimate of the value of the residue of your estate. Canadian tax rules can be complex at times and subject to interpretation. As well, there may be a number of planning opportunities available to reduce your final tax bill. I've listed a number of ideas in the following chapter.

You don't have to complete these worksheets or otherwise estimate today's value of the residue of your estate on your own. If you feel that you are getting bogged down trying to estimate the value of the residue of your estate, or trying to estimate your final tax bill (see the next chapter), your accountant or financial advisor should be able to help you with this, using their own software. They may even recommend projecting the value of the residue of your estate five, 10, or 20 years or more into the future.

ESTIMATING THE VALUE OF THE RESIDUE OF YOUR ESTATE

Date Completed   _____

Date Updated   _____

Step 1: Total up the value of all the assets to be transferred into your estate

All assets registered in your own name
(from the Assets worksheet) $_____

RRSPs/RRIF where "estate" is the beneficiary   +$_____

Life insurance where "estate" is the beneficiary   +$_____

Segregated funds where "estate" is the beneficiary   +$_____

Other assets where "estate" is the beneficiary   +$_____

Step 2: Subtract the value of bequests or gifts to be made according to the instructions in your will

Total value of bequests made in your will   – $_____

Total value of other gifts given in your will   – $_____

Step 3: Subtract the expenses to be paid out of your estate

From the worksheet on the next page   (C)   –$_____

Step 4: Calculate the value of the residue of your estate

Estimated Value of the Residue of your Estate   = $_____

TOTAL EXPENSES TO BE PAID OUT OF THE ESTATE (ESTIMATE)

The following amounts will be paid out of the value of your estate.

LIABILITIES/DEBTS

Credit card balances — $ _____

Lines of credit — + $ _____

Outstanding loans and/or promissory notes — + $ _____

Outstanding balances of mortgages and/or reverse mortgage — + $ _____

Other liabilities from liabilities worksheet — + $ _____

Total final income taxes (from (E) on page 147) — + $ _____

U.S. estate taxes — + $ _____

Continuing support payments (total value not insured) — + $ _____

OTHER COSTS OF DYING

Probate fee/tax (D from page 138) — + $ _____

Executor and trustee fees — + $ _____

Legal and accounting fees — + $ _____

Other professional fees — + $ _____

Funeral costs (if prepaid, enter 0) — + $ _____

Other final expenses and fees — + $ _____

Total debts and costs to be paid out of your estate (C) — = $ _____ *

*Use this figure for Estimating the Value of the Residue of Your Estate on page 135.

ESTIMATING YOUR PROBATE TAXES OR FEES

Probate taxes or fees are calculated on the value of your assets that flow through your will. In most provinces, do not include any assets that are registered as joint tenants with rights of survivorship or have a beneficiary designated. Some liabilities may be deducted from the value of your estate, such as a personal mortgage. For more information, talk to your accountant or your lawyer for the details of the rules in your province.

Date Completed   _____

Date Updated   _____

Probate Fees Across Canada *		Maximum
Alberta	$25 for the first $10,000 $100 on $10,001 to $25,000 $200 on $25,001 to $125,000 $300 on $125,001 to $250,000 $400 on amounts over $250,000	 $400
B.C.	$0 for estate under $10,000 $208 on $10,001 to $25,000 $6 per $1,000 on $25,001 to $50,000 $14 per $1,000 over $50,000	 none
Manitoba	$50 for first $10,000 plus $6 per $1,000 over $10,000	 none
New Brunswick	$25 up to $5,000 $50 on $5,001 to $10,000 $75 on $10,001 to $15,000 $100 on $15,001 to $20,000 $5 per $1,000 over $20,000	 none
Newfoundland	$75 plus $5 per $1,000 and $5 for each additional $1,000	 none
Nova Scotia	$70 up to $10,000 $150 on $10,001 to $25,000 $250 on $25,001 to $50,000 $700 on $50,001 to $100,000 over $100,000; $700 plus $12 per $1,000	 none
Ontario	$5 per $1,000 on first $50,000 $15 per $1,000 over $50,000	 none
PEI	$50 up to $10,000 $100 on estates $10,001 to $25,000 $200 on estates $25,001 to $50,000 $400 on $50,001 to $100,000 Over $100,000; $4 per $1,000	 none

Probate Fees Across Canada *		Maximum
Quebec	$0 for notarial will	$0
Saskatchewan	$7 for each $1,000	none
Yukon	$0 for estate under $25,000 $140 for estate over $25,000	$140
NWT Territories	$8 on the first $500 $15 on estate $501 to $1,000 Over $1,000; $3 per $1,000	none

Some provinces also charge relatively small "nuisance" fees for searches, making copies, etc.
*as of October 2001

SAMPLE PROBATE FEE CALCULATION

Here's a sample probate fee calculation for an estate valued at $200,000, based on the probate fee schedule for Nova Scotia.

For first $100,000	$ 700
On next $100,000	$1,200
Total	$1,900

Now estimate the cost of probating your will in your province using the information from the table above.

Value of all assets distributed according
to the instructions in your will $_____

Estimate of cost of probate   (D) $_____

Taxes

Death is one way you can have your name permanently removed from the Canada Customs and Revenue Agency's annual mailing list. But before that can happen, your executor has to recreate your tax life. It's your executor's job to complete your final tax return and settle up with the Canada Customs and Revenue Agency—before he or she distributes your estate to your beneficiaries. In this chapter, you'll also find a worksheet to summarize the details of your tax life and last, but not least, you'll find 51 ways to make sure you don't end up paying more tax or fees than necessary.

As well, in the event you become mentally incapacitated, your power of attorney or representative for financial decisions also have to recreate your tax life so they can file an annual tax return on your behalf.

TAX DETAILS WORKSHEET

Here's a worksheet you can use to summarize your tax situation.

Date Completed   _____

Date Updated   _____

YOUR INCOME TAX RETURNS

So where exactly do you keep those tax returns?

Year last filed: _____

Location of:

Last year's tax return(s):   _____

Notice of assessment for last year: _____

Tax returns for previous two years: _____

Notice of assessment for the two previous years: _____

Receipts for current year: _____

TAX RECEIPTS FOR THE CURRENT YEAR

Your representative will need to figure out your income from all sources for your income tax, as well as your deductions. A good starting point is last year's tax return.

❑   My sources of income for the current year are similar to the previous year
    (use my previous year's tax return as a model).

❑   My sources of income for the current year are similar to the previous year
    (use my previous year's tax return as a model), with the following exceptions.
    Check all that apply.

Stopped

❑   Receiving employment income

❑   Reduced my charitable donations

❑   Other: _____

❑   Other: _____

Started

- ❏ Home Buyers Plan
- ❏ LifeLong Learning Plan
- ❏ CPP benefits
- ❏ Old Age Security income
- ❏ RRIF income
- ❏ Annuity income
- ❏ Pension income
- ❏ Significant capital gains
- ❏ Additional charitable donations
- ❏ Major medical expenses
- ❏ Other: _____
- ❏ Other: _____

CAPITAL LOSSES

Have you ever had an investment that lost money? If you held that investment outside your RRSP or RRIF, you can claim eligible capital losses. While you are alive, capital losses can be deducted from capital gains, but on death, capital losses can be claimed against other types of income.

However, in order to use your capital losses, you are required to report them on your tax return in the year you realized the loss. Suppose you held 100 shares of Nortel that you bought at $100 (you weren't the only Canadian that paid $100 or more) and you sold them in 2001 for $40. You have a $6,000 loss and should report it on your 2001 tax return.

	Self	Partner
Do you have any unused capital losses?	❏ Yes ❏ No	❏ Yes ❏ No
Value of losses reported to CCRA*	$_____	$_____
Value of losses not yet reported to CCRA		
for previous years	$_____	$_____
for current tax year	$_____	$_____

Report them or risk losing them!

*Canada Customs and Revenue Agency (formerly Revenue Canada)

CHARITABLE DONATIONS

Yes   *No*

❑   ❑   Have you or your partner made any charitable donations that you have not yet claimed? If yes, complete the following.

Self/Partner	Year of Donation	Amount Donated	Amount Claimed to Date	Amount Not Yet Used
_____	_____	$_____	$_____	$_____
_____	_____	$_____	$_____	$_____
_____	_____	$_____	$_____	$_____

Charitable donations made in the five years before death, as well as donations made in the year of death, can be claimed on the final tax return, if they have not yet been claimed.

CAPITAL GAINS EXEMPTION

Yes   *No*

❑   ❑   If you or your partner declared any capital gains under the $100,000 capital gains declaration in 1994, do you have any amounts remaining that you have not used yet? If yes, complete the following.

Self/Partner	Asset	Amount Declared in 1994	Amount Claimed to Date	Amount Not Yet Used
_____	_____	$_____	$_____	$_____
_____	_____	$_____	$_____	$_____
_____	_____	$_____	$_____	$_____
_____	_____	$_____	$_____	$_____

Where is the $100,000 capital gains exemption form—the T664 or T664 (Seniors) election form (Election to Report a Capital Gain on Property Owned at the End of February 22, 1994) you filed in 1994?_____

Yes   *No*

❑   ❑   Did you own your home or other property prior to 1982?

Prior to 1982, Canadian residents could own more than one home and have it exempt from capital gains tax. Today, only the property deemed as a principal property is exempt from capital gains tax. If yes, where are the tax records for the value of these properties? _____

RECAPTURE

Yes *No*
❏ ❏   Will your estate have to report any recapture of the capital cost allowance (applies to assets which have been depreciated, such as computer equipment)? If yes, complete the following.

Self/Partner   Asset   Amount of Recapture

_____   _____ $ _____

_____   _____ $ _____

_____   _____ $ _____

CAPITAL GAINS EXEMPTION—$500,000

Yes *No*
❏ ❏   If you have a qualifying small business corporation, are you eligible to claim any capital gains under the $500,000 capital gains exemption? If you are not sure whether or not you are eligible, contact your accountant. If yes, complete the following.

Self/Partner   Asset   Amount Already Claimed

_____   _____ $ _____

_____   _____ $ _____

OTHER

Yes *No*
❏ ❏   Are there any assets (cottage, business, etc.) you do not want sold to pay any taxes that might be due?
If yes, what? _____

_____

OTHER TAX RETURNS

Yes *No*
❏ ❏   Have you ever, or are you currently, also filing a personal tax return in another country such as the U.S., or preparing a Canadian trust return? If yes, complete the following.

Type   Country

_____   _____

_____   _____

ESTIMATING YOUR FINAL TAX BILL

This worksheet is designed to provide a "quick and dirty" estimate of what your final tax bill might be. However, this estimate is highly simplified and is designed as just a starting point, but it could help you and your advisors determine whether or not some of the more complex estate planning strategies might be appropriate. If you prefer, you could estimate the final tax bill using tax software you currently may have, such as CANTAX or QuickTax. But be sure not to e-file it!

I recommend you obtain a copy of the "Preparing Returns for Deceased Persons" and a copy of the "General Income Tax and Benefit Return" from Canada Customs and Revenue Agency (CCRA formerly Revenue Canada) and use them to help you estimate your final tax bill. This information can be obtained from any CCRA office or online at www.ccra-adrc.gc.ca.

Date Completed   _____

Date Updated   _____

Step 1: Estimate your taxable income for the year of death, assuming you died tomorrow

Current income

      Employment   + $_____

      CPP income   + $_____

      CPP death benefit (maximum value $2,500)   + $_____

      OAS   + $_____

      Self-employment   + $_____

      Rental income   + $_____

      Other pension income   + $_____

      Other   + $_____

Interest and dividend income

      Interest income   + $_____

      Dividend income   + $_____

Registered plans (RRSPs, RRIF)

      Withdrawals from RRSPs, RRIFS   + $_____

      Value of plan on date of death where the beneficiary is "estate"   + $_____

Value of plan on date of death where the beneficiary is not a spouse, common-law partner, or eligible child   + $_____

Outstanding balance of Home Buyers Plan   + $_____

Outstanding balance of LifeLong Learning Plan   + $_____

Capital gains

    Taxable capital gains   + $_____

Other income   + $_____

Total Income   = $_____

Less

    RRSP contributions already made to your own or spousal RRSP, or to be made to a spousal RRSP after your death   – $_____

    Stock option deductions   – $_____

    Net capital losses from previous years   – $_____

    Remaining amounts from T664 declared in 1994   – $_____

    Other deductions   – $_____

Taxable income   = $_____

Step 2: Estimate the amount of federal income tax due

Some people will say that combined, the federal and provincial income tax on death will be about 50% of your taxable income. However, using 50% would over-estimate the tax bill, since Canadians only pay federal tax at the top tax rate when their taxable income is more than about $100,000. The federal tax brackets at the time of writing were as follows:

Federal Income Tax Brackets	
Taxable Income	Tax Rate
Under $31,677	16%
$31,677 to $63,354	22%
$63,354 to $103,000	26%
over $103,000	29%
*as of January 1, 2002	

These tax brackets are now fully linked to inflation and will increase as the consumer price index (CPI) increases.

Example:

Suppose your taxable income is $200,000 on death. The amount of your federal tax could be estimated as:

Taxable Income	Income in Bracket		Tax Rate		Federal Tax Due
First $31,677	$ 31,677	x	.16	=	$ 5,068
From $31,677 to $63,354	$ 31,677	x	.22	=	$ 6,969
From $63,354 to $103,000	$ 39,646	x	.26	=	$10,308
over $103,000	$ 97,000	x	.29	=	$28,130
Totals	$200,000*				$50,475

This amount should equal the total taxable income.

You can now estimate the amount of federal tax that might be due assuming you died tomorrow.

Taxable Income	Income in Bracket		Tax Rate		Federal Tax Due
First $31,677	_____	x	.16	=	$ _____
From $31,677 to $63,354	_____	x	.22	=	$ _____
From $63,354 to $103,000	_____	x	.26	=	$ _____
over $103,000	_____	x	.29	=	$ _____
Totals	_____ *			(A)	$ _____

This amount should equal your total taxable income.

Step 3: Estimate the amount of provincial income tax due

However, federal tax is not the only income tax Canadians pay. We also have to pay provincial tax. But almost every province uses its own income tax brackets and tax rates. Some calculate the amount of tax based on your taxable income; others based the calculation on the amount of federal tax you owe. At the lower end of the scale, provincial tax rates in B.C. in 2002 were:

Taxable Income	Tax Rate
$0-$31,124	6.05%
$31,124-$62,249	9.15%
$62,249-$71,470	11.7%
$71,470-$86,785	13.7%
over $86,785	14.7%

At the higher end of the scale, the provincial tax rates in Quebec in 2002 were:

Taxable Income	Tax Rate
$0-$26,000	16%
$26,001-$52,000	20%
over $52,000	24%

In Alberta, the provincial tax is levied at a flat rate of 9.5% on your taxable income for the year.

If you are in a province with higher provincial tax rates, you could estimate the amount of provincial income tax to be approximately 50% of the amount of federal tax bill. In a province such as Alberta, you could estimate the amount of provincial tax to be 9.5% of your taxable income.

Estimate of provincial income tax due   (B) $ _____

Step 4: Estimate the combined federal and provincial taxes due

Estimate of federal income tax due   (A) $ _____

Estimate of provincial income tax due   (B) $ _____

Total final income tax estimated   (E) $ _____ *

Use this figure on the "Total Expenses to be Paid Worksheet" on page 136.

Of course, any non-refundable tax credits you will be eligible to claim on the final tax return, such as the basic personal credit, age amount, spousal amount, disability amount, tuition credit, medical expenses and charitable donations and gifts, etc. will reduce the amount of tax owing.

Remember, this estimate is very simplified. For more accuracy, or to project the future tax bill, contact your accountant or financial advisor.

FIFTY-ONE WAYS TO REDUCE THE COST OF DYING

On death, there are taxes and fees to be paid as part of settling up your financial affairs. While it's up to your executor to total the costs and pay for them out of your estate, with careful planning you may be able to reduce the cost of dying and leave a larger estate.

Here are 51 ideas that have been proven to reduce the cost of dying and leave more for your beneficiaries.

Here are some estate planning ideas to reduce income taxes that:

• can be implemented while you are alive

• implemented by your executor—provided you have given him or her the powers in your will to do so

• let your beneficiaries keep more of what they earn after they receive their inheritance. (Your beneficiaries receive the inheritance tax-free—provided your estate has settled your accounts with CCRA. But any future interest, dividend, or capital gains is taxable.)

I've also included estate planning ideas to reduce the U.S. estate tax bill and other costs of dying.

Not all of these ideas will apply to everyone. Some of the ideas presented here will work together, others will not, and you and your advisors will have to determine which ones might be the most effective for you. For example, owning assets jointly with your spouse with rights of survivorship can reduce the cost of probating a will, but this form of ownership is not compatible with setting up a spousal testamentary trust. But since there can be set-up costs and annual expenses related to administering some of these strategies on an ongoing basis, be sure to factor in these expenses—they would reduce the potential savings.

On page 172, you'll find a section titled "Ideas to Discuss." You can use this to note any tax minimization strategy which you would use to explore in more detail with your own professional advisors. Keep in mind that these are ideas only and are not to be construed as advice for your personal situation.

Ways to Reduce the Final Tax Bill

1. Name your spouse or common-law partner as the named beneficiary of your registered assets (RRSPs, RRIFs). Partner refers to a common-law partner of the same or opposite sex.

2. Name your "estate" as the beneficiary of your RRSPs and RRIFs and give your executor the power in your will to elect to transfer some or all of your RRSP/RRIF to a registered plan on behalf of your spouse or partner

after your death. This could give your executor added flexibility at the time of death and be useful if you have tax credits or deductions or capital losses that might otherwise go unused, or if you are in a low income tax bracket in the year of death.

3. Name your children or grandchildren as the beneficiary of your RRSP or RRIF. Transfers of these registered accounts to children or grandchildren under certain conditions (i.e., if he or she is financially dependent or physically or mentally infirm) can be tax effective.

4. Leave assets that have earned capital gains—that you have not yet paid the tax on—to a spouse or common-law partner to take advantage of the spousal rollover.

5. Make withdrawals from your RRSP before you turn 69, if you are in a lower tax bracket now than you expect to be in the year of death, to take advantage of your lower tax rate.

6. Withdraw more than the minimum from your RRIFs if you are in a lower tax bracket now than you expect you will be in the year of death, to take advantage of your lower tax rate.

7. Negotiate with your employer to receive up to $10,000 in death benefits on a tax-free basis.

8. Trigger some capital gains sooner (sell, transfer or gift) rather than later if you are in a lower tax bracket now than you expect you will be in the year of death, to take advantage of your lower tax rate.

9. Calculate your adjusted cost base (or have your accountant do it) for your property and investments held outside your RRSP and RRIFs. Your adjusted cost base normally includes what you paid for the investment (or its value when you received it, if it was a gift) plus any expenses to acquire it, such as commissions or legal fees, plus the cost of any improvements or capital expenditures.

10. Make a charitable gift and use the tax receipt to reduce your tax bill. To save even more tax, gift assets in kind by donating stocks, bonds, or mutual funds that have increased in value, rather than giving cash. In addition to claiming the charitable tax receipt, you would then only have to pay tax on 25% of the profits (the capital gain), rather than the usual 50%.

11. If you own more than one piece of property (such as a house and a vacation property), designate the property with the most capital gains as your principal residence.

12. Don't forget any amounts you have remaining under the $100,000 capital gains exemption you may have declared in 1994. File your T664 or

T664 (Seniors) election form (Election to Report a Capital Gain on Property Owned at the End of February 22, 1994) with your will or this workbook.

13. Implement an estate freeze by transferring assets into a closely held corporation. An estate freeze effectively freezes the market value of the assets and allows the tax on the future growth to be deferred, without requiring tax to be paid on that growth on the death of the original owner.

14. Transfer assets into an inter vivos trust. A living trust offers control as to when the tax is paid—death does not have to trigger the tax.

Ways Your Executor Can Reduce Your Final Tax Bill

15. File more than one tax return. Your executor can file up to three returns in addition to your final tax return: 1) a tax return for rights and things, 2) for sole proprietorship income, and 3) income from a trust. Certain amounts can be claimed in full on each return, including the basic personal amount, age amount, and the spousal amount. To further reduce the overall tax bill, other amounts, such as disability amount, charitable donations, and medical expenses can be split between the final return and optional returns.

16. Claim medical expenses incurred in the last 24-month period (longer than the usual 12-months) that have not been claimed previously.

17. Determine if it is more beneficial to claim attendant or nursing home care as a medical expense or as a disability amount.

18. If all the charitable receipts can not be used on the final tax return, request that the deceased's tax return for the previous year be adjusted to use up as much of the charitable receipts there as possible.

19. File the tax return on time so the estate is not charged any tax penalties or interest for filing late.

20. Rather than reporting CPP or QPP death benefits on the final tax return, elect to file this amount on the T3 Trust return for the estate, if this results in a lower overall tax bill.

21. Elect to transfer assets to your spouse or partner as a spousal rollover, but consider transferring them at the deceased's adjusted cost base, at a higher cost base (up to fair market value) or somewhere in between, to use up any remaining capital losses, or to maximize the value of charitable receipts, if the deceased was in a low tax bracket, etc.

CHAPTER 7 • *Taxes*

CHAPTER 7 • *Taxes* 151

22. If the deceased has unused RRSP contributions and a spouse or partner who is 69 or younger, make a final contribution to a spousal RRSP and use the deduction on the final tax return.

23. If the deceased had amounts owing under the RRSP Home Buyers' Plan or the Lifelong Learning Plan and a surviving spouse or common-law partner, elect jointly with spouse to continue to make the repayments.

24. Rather than selling assets at a reduced market price to pay the tax bill, consider electing to pay the tax bill (plus interest at the prescribed rate) in up to 10 annual tax installments. This could help preserve the value of the estate.

25. After capital losses have been claimed against capital gains, use any remaining capital losses to reduce other income on the final tax return and/or the return for the previous year.

26. If assets fall in value while they are held in the estate and the executor sells the portfolio during the estate's first year, the loss can be applied to the deceased's final tax return.

27. Ask for a Tax Clearance Certificate when the tax returns have been filed, taxes paid, and the assessment notices received, so you know that CCRA has closed the books on the deceased's tax returns and that no further tax needs to be paid.

If You Are a Business or Farm Owner

28. Determine if, and how, you can take advantage of the enhanced $500,000 capital gains exemption for qualified small business corporations.

29. If you own a qualified farm property, consider transferring it to a spouse, partner, child or grandchild, or spouse of a child or grandchild.

30. Distribute the assets according to a shareholder agreement, rather than a will.

Ways to Reduce the Cost Of Probating Your Will

Probate is calculated on the value of the assets that are distributed according to the instructions in your will. If you live in a province where probate taxes or fees are relatively low, some of the more complex strategies will likely cost more to implement than they save. However, in provinces where the probate taxes are relatively high with no maximum, if you have a relatively large estate, you may want to explore these ideas to see if they might work for your situation.

Anything you can do to distribute assets outside of the will, such as naming beneficiaries when applicable, will reduce the cost of probating your estate.

31. Own assets jointly with rights of survivorship with your spouse or partner.

32. Give assets or cash to adult beneficiaries while you are alive, provided you don't need them.

33. Name a beneficiary on your life insurance policies and segregated fund contracts.

34. Name a beneficiary on your RRSPs and RRIFs.

35. Name a beneficiary on your employer pension plan.

36. If you have a company or trust, consider making it a resident in a province with lower probate taxes/fees.

37. Prepare a will for those assets that need probating and a separate will for those that do not.

38. If you have assets in different provinces with different probate fee schedules, prepare two wills, one for the assets in each province.

39. If you are 65 or older, transfer your assets into an alter ego trust or a joint spousal trust.

40. And my personal favourite, spend a little more of your money while you are alive.

Ways to Reduce U.S. Estate Tax

The Internal Revenue Service taxes an estate based on its worldwide value at the time of death (not just your profits!). CCRA taxes your profits and the value of your RRSPs and RRIFs at the time of death. While Canadian residents may obtain some relief from double taxation if the total estate is less than $1.2 million with a relatively small percentage of the estate held in the U.S., here are some ideas to reduce any potential U.S. estate tax bill. If you don't own U.S. property at the time of your death, your estate will not pay any U.S. estate taxes.

41. Make small, regular gifts of U.S. property (although this is not practical if your only U.S. asset is a condo worth $150,000).

42. Sell your U.S. assets and property prior to death. Suppose you're not using the condo as much as you used to; sell the property while you are alive and move the money back to Canada.

43. Hold U.S. investments (but not personal real estate) inside a Canadian corporation. However, it may be determined in the future that these assets are not really corporate assets, which would limit the effectiveness of this strategy.

44. Leave property to your Canadian spouse to take advantage of the spousal credit.

45. Spend or give away assets to make your estate worth less than US$1.2 million.

Maximize Future Income Splitting

46. Rather than leaving an inheritance outright to any beneficiary, leave some or all of the inheritance in a testamentary trust, a trust set up according to the instructions in your will. Although future income splitting is not the only reason for setting up a testamentary trust, a testamentary trust is taxed at graduated rates as a separate taxpayer.

Ways to Reduce Other Fees and Expenses

47. Execute a proper will so your estate does not to have to apply to (and pay for) the courts to have an administrator appointed to settle your estate.

48. Prepare an affidavit of execution, or similar document, at the time the will is signed and witnessed to certify the will was properly executed, so that the witnesses do not need to be tracked down after your death.

49. If you need the services of a corporate trustee to settle your estate, shop around for the services you need at a cost you are willing to pay. Don't be afraid to try to negotiate the executor fees.

50. To reduce courier and photocopying charges, transfer share certificates currently in your safety deposit box to an investment account with a broker or financial planning firm. On your death, your executor would then only have to send the supporting documentation once—a copy of the will, a copy of the death certificate, and a copy of the grant or letters of probate, as required—to the brokerage firm to have them re-registered in the name of the estate.

51. Preplan your funeral so your executor and family do not make expensive decisions quickly.

CHAPTER EIGHT

Additional Worksheets

If you've been working through this workbook from the beginning, you'll have completed many worksheets, all of which have been designed to help you consider your estate plan and make it easier for the people you name in your documents—power of attorney for financial decisions, power of attorney for personal and health care decisions, and executor in your will—to make decisions on your behalf and carry out your instructions.

You've worked through much of the "who," "what," "how," and even estimated the "how much" of your estate plan. You may be wondering "what else is there to consider?"

In this chapter, you'll find worksheets to help you:

1. estimate the amount of life insurance you might need, and

2. consider your funeral wishes and how you would like to be remembered.

Some people may find they have enough life insurance in place and others may find they have too little to take care of those they leave behind or realize their estate planning objectives. The life insurance worksheet lets you consider the current value of your estate, the assets that are to be left to your spouse, costs, fees, and taxes that would be deducted from the value of your estate and any amounts that are earmarked for special purposes. It also considers the annual income your dependents might need after your death, the income they might receive from all sources, and the amount of capital needed to fund the difference.

The funeral planning worksheet can be used to consider those issues that are important to you regarding your funeral, whether they reflect your customs or personal preferences.

In Chapter 9, you'll work through the "where" of your estate plan, where you keep all your important personal papers, so they can be located when needed.

LIFE INSURANCE WORKSHEET

The amount of life insurance you require depends on your situation (the number and needs of your dependents and business partners). The calculation considers the amount of insurance you currently have in place, the assets you have, your debts, executor and probate fees, income taxes due on death, education funding, other sources of income your survivors may have, and some assumptions about the future.

Some people think they have too much life insurance; others too little. But if a bus hit you tomorrow, would your survivors have enough money to pay the bills, finish their education, or just enough to live on? Will there be enough money to create the income they require? If a bus hit your spouse or partner, would you have enough?

You can use this worksheet to estimate the amount of life insurance coverage that you and your spouse or common-law partner might need. Refer to the assets worksheets and the liability worksheets, as well as the cost of dying worksheets to help you here.

Date Completed   _____

Date Updated   _____

Step 1: Start with the amount of capital you expect will be available after your death

The value of assets in your name only
(GICs, bank accounts, investment accounts, etc.) $_____

The value of your RRSP/RRIF where "estate" is the beneficiary   + $_____

The death benefit or commuted value of your
your pension plan where "estate" is the beneficiary   + $_____

Death benefit from CPP or QPP (maximum $2,500)   + $_____

The death benefit from insurance you currently have
where "estate" is the beneficiary (include group insurance)
less any policy loans   + $_____

Commuted value of any annuity payments remaining under
any remaining guaranteed period   + $_____

Other assets registered in your name only, that could be
sold on your death   + $_____

Step 2: Add in the value of the assets your spouse will receive on your death

Assets registered jointly with your spouse   + $_____

The value of your RRSP/RRIF where your spouse is
the beneficiary   + $_____

The death benefit or commuted value of your
pension plan where your spouse is the beneficiary   + $_____

The commuted value of any remaining annuity payments still
within the guarantee period where your spouse is the beneficiary   + $_____

The death benefit from insurance where
your spouse is the beneficiary   + $_____

Amount of capital available   = $_____

Step 3: Deduct what will have to be paid on your death

Uninsured debts that will need to be paid in full
(mortgage, loans, credit cards, etc.)   − $_____

Canadian income tax due on death ((E) from Chapter 7)   − $_____

U.S. estate taxes due on death   − $_____

Probate taxes/fees ((D) from Chapter 6)   − $_____

Funeral costs   − $_____

Legal and other professional fees   − $_____

Other final expenses   − $_____

Net amount of capital available   = $_____

Step 4: Deduct lump-sum amounts required for special purposes

From the net amount of capital available, deduct the amounts you estimate will be required to fund any lump-sum items, such as establishing an emergency fund, paying for your children's education, or gifts to other family members or charity.

Present value of amount needed to fund your
children's education   − $_____

Amount needed to establish an emergency fund
(estimate a minimum of three months' expenses)   − $_____

Bequests and cash you want to gift to beneficiaries,
who are not your dependents, or to charity   − $_____

Other purpose: _____   − $_____

Other purpose: _____   − $_____

Capital available/shortfall after lump sums spent   (F) = $_____

If this amount is negative, you have a shortfall of capital available to fund your final expenses and/or to fund your lump-sum items.

Step 5: Estimate the annual income your dependents will need after your death

Start with the income your family will need to support their lifestyle. Then determine how much income they might have and then estimate how much capital will be needed to generate the difference.

Annual expenses for your family's lifestyle

Accommodation (rent, property taxes, condo fees, etc.)	$_____
Utility costs	$_____
Property insurance	$_____
Communications (phone, cable, internet, etc.)	$_____
Recreational property	$_____
Transportation (car, public transit, taxis, etc.)	$_____
Food (groceries, dining out)	$_____
Clothing	$_____
Personal care	$_____
Health care (drugs, dental, alternative, etc.)	$_____
Vacations	$_____
Entertainment	$_____
Alcohol and cigarettes	$_____
Clubs/Associations	$_____
Gifts	$_____
Allowance for children	$_____
Childcare (daycare, babysitting, summer camp, etc.)	$_____
Charitable donations	$_____
Income taxes	$_____

Annual Income Needed to Support Family's Lifestyle   (G) = $_____

Estimate the pre-tax annual income your dependents will receive after your death.

Spouse's employment income	$_____
Survivor pension income	$_____
Spouse's investment income	$_____
Spouse's income from RRIF/Annuity	$_____
Survivor CPP/QPP income	$_____
GST Rebate/Child Tax Credit	$_____
Dependent Survivor CPP/QPP Income	$_____

Other sources of income: _____ $_____

Anticipated Annual Income   (H) = $_____

Calculate the annual income surplus/shortfall

Annual income surplus/shortfall   G-H = $_____ *

* If this amount is negative, you may want to eliminate the shortfall by purchasing additional life insurance to protect your family's lifestyle or revisit the bequests and cash you want to gift to beneficiaries who are not your dependents, or to charity.

Step 6: Estimate the amount of capital or life insurance you may require

a) Estimate the amount needed to fund the annual income shortfall, if any, from Step 5.

How much capital, invested at today's rates, is needed to generate the additional income required each year? You need to consider the inflation rate, the rate of return that realistically can be expected, the number of years that the income would be required, and the tax rate of the person receiving the income. The higher the rate of return you expect you would be able to make, the less life insurance that would be required.

To estimate the amount of capital required, start by dividing the income you need by the rate of return currently being offered on 5-year GICs:

- If GICs are currently earning 4%, divide the annual income needed by .04.

- If GICs are currently earning 3%, divide the annual income needed by .03.

If you anticipate the portfolio would be invested in a mix of fixed income investments and stocks, you might want to use a higher projected rate of return.

For example, if your family will need an additional $20,000 a year for the rest of their life and it would be reasonable to expect to earn an average of 5% a year over the long term, the amount of life insurance needed might be estimated as follows:

$$\frac{\$20,000}{.05} = \$400,000$$

Using your numbers, the amount of capital required to produce
the income needed is approximately: $_____

b) Add in the amount of any shortfall in capital, if any, from Step 4 (F).   + $_____

c) Deduct the amount of capital currently available, if any, from Step 4 (F).   – $_____

An estimate of the additional amount of life insurance needed
is approximately   = $_____

**This is an estimate of the amount of life insurance you need. This estimate could be further refined by considering how many years this income will be needed and whether or not the capital could also be used to fund the income needed, etc. This worksheet does not include insurance you may require for any business needs.

FUNERAL PLANNING WORKSHEET

Death is never an easy topic to discuss. While the final responsibility for arranging your funeral lies with your executor, you can leave specific instructions or provide general guidance regarding your wishes to assist your family and executor. Many people are reluctant to consider the funeral decisions that need to be made, either by them or by family on their behalf. Here's a funeral planning worksheet.

❑ I have discussed my funeral wishes with my executor

I would like to be:

❑ buried   ❑ cremated   ❑ doesn't matter

I would like the funeral or memorial service to be:

❑ simple   ❑ elaborate   ❑ doesn't matter

I would like my funeral or memorial service to:

❑ reflect my religious beliefs _____

❑ be non-denominational

❑ non-religious

❑ doesn't matter

I would like:

❑ the service to be conducted by _____

❑ music to be played: _____ by_____

❑ passage to be read: _____ by_____

❑ _____ to conduct the service.

I would like:

❑ flowers

❑ instead of flowers, donations to be made to _____

I: ❑ want   ❑ don't want   an open casket.

If cremated, I want my ashes to be:

❑ buried at: _____

❑ scattered at: _____

❑ other: _____

❑ I have pre-arranged my funeral through:

Name of funeral company: _____

Address: _____

Phone no.: _____

If you have also pre-paid your funeral, include the:

Contract no.: _____

Other special instructions:

_____

_____

_____

_____

Do you want to make any arrangement to pay for the funeral/cremation/burial?

❑ Yes ❑ No If no:

      ❑ request a family member pay the expenses and authorize your estate to reimburse them?

      ❑ authorize your executor to pay the cost from the estate?

      ❑ use a small insurance policy?

      ❑ other: _____

      ❑ prepay the funeral with the funeral home?

QUESTIONS TO ASK BEFORE PREPAYING YOUR FUNERAL:

If the funeral arranged actually costs more than the value of the contract, who is responsible for the difference?
❑ your estate ❑ the funeral home

If the funeral arranged costs less than the value of the contract, will the difference be:
❑ refunded? ❑ not refunded?

If the funeral is conducted somewhere else, will the value of the contract be:
❑ fully refunded? ❑ partially refunded? ❑ not refunded?

If you have to cancel the contract, will you receive:
❑ a full refund? ❑ a partial refund? ❑ no refund?

QUESTIONS TO ASK BEFORE PAYING FOR A CEMETERY PLOT:

Yes   *No*

❑   ❑   Will you have the right to put a memorial on the site?

❑   ❑   Are there any restrictions on the type or style of monument?

❑   ❑   How many caskets are permitted in each grave?

❑   ❑   If you or your executor cancels the contract, will you receive a refund?

WHAT DO YOU WANT THEM TO SAY ABOUT YOU WHEN YOU ARE GONE?

❑   I've attached suggestions for my obituary.

_____

_____

_____

_____

_____

_____

_____

_____

"Now go out and live your life
as you would like to be remembered!"

CHAPTER NINE

Locating Your Important Papers

Who was it that said we were moving to a paperless society? I don't know about you, but I have more personal paperwork today than I have ever had. This chapter helps you organize the "where" of your estate plan.

So where do you keep all your personal documents? In a drawer? In a box in the basement? In a safe? In your safety deposit box? Somewhere else? Some people keep their important papers in such a "safe" place that not even their executor can find them! When the time comes, your family and representatives need to be able to find all the relevant paperwork.

LOCATION OF PERSONAL DOCUMENTS WORKSHEET

Use this worksheet to detail the documents you have and where they are located. Don't worry about any item that does not apply to you—just leave it blank. If you need more space to record the information for you and your spouse/partner, feel free to make photocopies of the pages you require for your own personal use.

Location of birth certificates: _____

Location of citizenship papers: _____

Location of adoption papers: _____

Driver's Licence no.:_____Prov/State:_____Expiry date:_____Location:_____

Health Card no.:_____ Location: _____

Social Insurance no. (SIN): _____ Location: _____

Social Security no. (US): _____ Location: _____

Passport no.: _____ Country : _____ Location: _____

For each item below, indicate if you have one, and if so, where you keep the original document and supporting paperwork.

Yes	No		Document(s) are located at:
☐	☐	Marriage certificate	_____
☐	☐	Marriage contract	_____
☐	☐	Co-habitation agreement	_____
☐	☐	Separation agreement	_____
☐	☐	Divorce agreement	_____
☐	☐	Name change paperwork	_____
☐	☐	Bankruptcy paperwork?	_____
☐	☐	Will?	_____
☐	☐	Codicil	_____

Yes No

❑ ❑   Power of attorney for property/financial affairs/mandate/representative agreement

      Date prepared: _____ Location: _____

      Names of everyone who has a copy: _____

❑ ❑   A separate power of attorney in effect at any financial institution

      Financial institution: _____ Address: _____

      Financial institution: _____ Address: _____

      Financial institution: _____ Address: _____

❑ ❑   Power of attorney (POA) for personal care or health care

      Date prepared: _____ Location: _____

      Names of everyone who has a copy: _____

❑ ❑   Separate living will

      Date prepared: _____ Location: _____

❑ ❑   Other advance medical directive

      Date prepared: _____ Location: _____

❑ ❑   Organ/tissue donation form or donor card

      Date prepared: _____ Location: _____

❑ ❑   Trust(s) currently in effect (living trust, alter ego trust, family trust, etc.)

      Name of trust: _____ Location: _____

      Name of trust: _____ Location: _____

      Name of trust: _____ Location: _____

❑ ❑   Employment benefit statement and booklet

      Location: _____

❑ ❑   Employment contract

      Location: _____

❑ ❑   Prearranged funeral agreement

      Location: _____

Yes	No	
❑	❑	Title to cemetery plot or mausoleum

Location of deed: _____

| ❑ | ❑ | Are you a war veteran? |

Location of service/discharge papers and service record: _____

| ❑ | ❑ | RRSP/Locked-in RRSP/Group RRSP/etc. statements |

Location of statements: _____

| ❑ | ❑ | RRIF/LIF, etc., statements |

Location of statements: _____

| ❑ | ❑ | Investment statements |

Location of statements: _____

| ❑ | ❑ | Stock or bond certificates |

Location of certificates: _____

| ❑ | ❑ | Statement of segregated fund holdings |

Location of statements: _____

| ❑ | ❑ | Life insurance policies |

Location: _____ Date last reviewed: _____

| ❑ | ❑ | Disability insurance policies |

Location: _____ Date last reviewed: _____

| ❑ | ❑ | Household accounts: |

Where do you keep all the records related to running your home (utility statements, condo fees, property taxes, cable, phone and internet services, etc.)?

Location: _____

| ❑ | ❑ | Other: _____ |

Location: _____

Yes No
❑   ❑   Loyalty Programs

	Program Name	Account No.
Credit card	_____	_____
	_____	_____
	_____	_____
	_____	_____
Store	_____	_____
	_____	_____
	_____	_____
	_____	_____
Travel	_____	_____
(air, train, hotel, etc.)	_____	_____
	_____	_____
	_____	_____

❑   ❑   Memberships (health, golf, fitness, etc.)

	Description	Membership No.
	_____	_____
	_____	_____
	_____	_____
	_____	_____

Yes　*No*

❏　❏　Professional Associations, Clubs, Other Memberships

Description	Membership No.
_____	_____
_____	_____
_____	_____
_____	_____

❏　❏　Other: _____

　　　　Location: _____

❏　❏　Other: _____

　　　　Location: _____

LOCATION OF BUSINESS DOCUMENTS WORKSHEET

If you have a sole proprietorship or a partnership, it's quite possible that your expense receipts for the current year are thrown in a box or a drawer, waiting for you to have time to organize them.

The information in this section, combined with the assets of your business (found in an earlier form), will not provide your executor with all the information they need to know to settle up your business—they might sell it or close the doors—but it will help them find any key documents you have, so they are not grasping at straws.

One of the first calls they will make regarding your business is to call your accountant and/or lawyer, so be sure you've included their names in the Contact Section, found earlier in the workbook.

Yes No

❑ ❑ Payroll records

Location: _____

❑ ❑ Partnership/Shareholder agreement(s)

Location: _____

❑ ❑ Buy/Sell agreement(s)

Location: _____

❑ ❑ Financial statements for the business or farm

Location: _____

❑ ❑ Tax returns

Location: _____

❑ ❑ GST/HST records

Location: _____

❑ ❑ Provincial Retail Sales Tax records

Location: _____

❑ ❑ Corporate seal

Location: _____

❑ ❑ Minute book

Location: _____

❑ ❑ Other: _____

Location: _____

A Final Word

Nothing stays the same.

These worksheets reflect your financial, tax, and estate plan at one point in time and were designed to help you organize your thoughts and detail your records. If you worked through them all, you should now be more organized than you were when you started and better prepared to consult with your lawyer, accountant, and/or financial advisor. Working with a professional who understands your personal situation can help make sure you don't miss any opportunities and ensure that your estate planning strategies produce the results you want, even if it means you need to take steps to revise parts of your estate plan.

If you find you've ended up with a more complex estate plan than you'd ever imagined, consider "if there is a simpler, more cost-effective solution" that would achieve your objectives. If it's so complex you have trouble following it, imagine how your executor might feel.

I invite you to read *You Can't Take It With You: The Common-Sense Guide to Estate Planning*, the main book to this companion workbook, if you have not already done so.

I wish I could tell you that you only had to plan your estate once. But your priorities and family members will change over time, and you may have to revise and update your estate plan so you don't pay any more in tax than is absolutely necessary. You also don't want to miss changing legislation that could impact your estate plan. That said, I recommend that you build enough features into your estate plan so it will "wear" as well as it can. For example, have you named backups for your executor, guardian, and power or attorney or other representative, so if the person named is unwilling or unable to act when the time comes, you already have an alternate? It's also important to build your estate plan so it will distribute your estate the way you want it, regardless of the value of your assets, debts, or tax bill down the road.

If you have any suggestions for forms and worksheets you would find useful in future editions, I invite you to e-mail them to me at fosters@whosmindingyourmoney.com. If you are the first person to submit a suggestion that I use in a future edition of the workbook, I'll send you a free copy of the updated workbook.

"Dream as if you'll live forever;
Live as if you'll die tomorrow."
—James Dean

IDEAS TO DISCUSS

With my spouse/partner/family

_____

_____

_____

With my lawyer

_____

_____

_____

With my financial advisor/planner

_____

_____

_____

With my insurance agent

_____

_____

_____

With my accountant

_____

_____

_____

With my banker or trust officer

_____

_____

_____

Appendix A

LIST OF DUTIES FOR AN EXECUTOR OR ESTATE TRUSTEE

People used to consider it an honour to be asked to be an estate trustee or an executor for a friend or family member. Anyone who has ever acted as an executor will confirm that it is a job, and sometimes not a well paid job at that. An executor has to be prepared to write lots of letters and deal with lawyers, Canada Customs and Revenue Agency, insurance companies, real estate agents, business valuators, former employers, creditors, accountants, beneficiaries, and other interested parties, as well as the deceased's professional advisors.

Although the funeral home and other people you might have to deal with will provide advice and guidance, it is the executor's job to follow through on his or her duties to ensure that all items are completed.

If you are the executor of an estate, the following checklist outlines some of your duties. However, the administration and settling of estates varies across the country. The following is for educational purposes only and is not to be considered as tax, financial, or legal advice.

EXECUTOR CHECKLIST

Started   *Completed*   *Not Applicable*

General

Started	Completed	Not Applicable	
❑	❑	❑	Arrange the funeral and cremation or burial of the deceased.
❑	❑	❑	Obtain the death certificate and certified copies.
❑	❑	❑	Locate and review the instructions in the original will.
❑	❑	❑	Meet with the lawyer that will represent the estate in all legal matters.
❑	❑	❑	Submit an application to the provincial court for the Probate Certificate or Grant of Probate.
❑	❑	❑	Arrange probate fees or taxes to be paid to the provincial court.
❑	❑	❑	Locate all beneficiaries, including charities, and notify them that they have an interest in the estate under the terms of the will.
❑	❑	❑	Explain your role to the beneficiaries.
❑	❑	❑	Notify the spouse of any entitlement he or she may have under family law, and recommend the spouse receive independent legal advice, if necessary.
❑	❑	❑	Deal with any claims dependents may have under provincial dependent relief provisions.
❑	❑	❑	Keep the beneficiaries informed as to the progress of administering the estate.
❑	❑	❑	Review all personal papers of the deceased to help locate the deceased's assets and debts, key contacts, tax information, etc.

Deal with Government Benefit Programs

Started	Completed	Not Applicable	
❑	❑	❑	Cancel Old Age Security benefits.
❑	❑	❑	Contact the Income Security Office to stop CPP cheques (or the Quebec Pension Plan Office to stop QPP cheques).
❑	❑	❑	Apply to CPP/QPP for any death benefits the deceased qualifies for.
❑	❑	❑	Apply to CPP/QPP for any surviving spouse and dependent pension benefits.
❑	❑	❑	Contact Human Resources Development Canada to cancel the deceased's Social Insurance Number (SIN).

Started	*Completed*	*Not Applicable*	
❏	❏	❏	Contact the social security office in the U.S. to stop benefits.
❏	❏	❏	Apply to the social security office in the U.S. to apply for any death or survivor benefits.
❏	❏	❏	If the deceased is retired from the military, contact the appropriate veteran's office to receive any application benefits.

Obtain all Benefits Payable to the Estate

❏	❏	❏	Contact all service clubs and veterans clubs for death benefits that may be payable to the estate.
❏	❏	❏	Obtain all unpaid wages and other benefits from the deceased's former employer.
❏	❏	❏	Contact all of the deceased's employers (current and former) to determine if any pension or survivor benefits exist.
❏	❏	❏	Apply for any amounts payable to the estate under life insurance policies.
❏	❏	❏	Determine the options available for any remaining pension plans or annuities, and determine if the monthly income should continue, or the commuted value be paid out.

Manage the Assets of the Estate

❏	❏	❏	Prepare a detailed inventory of the deceased's assets, including the contents of the deceased's safety deposit box.
❏	❏	❏	Locate all bank accounts of the deceased, and determine the balance on deposit for each account. Notify the financial institutions of the death.
❏	❏	❏	Search for any unclaimed bank accounts.
❏	❏	❏	Open a bank account for the estate and transfer the deceased's bank accounts to the estate bank account.
❏	❏	❏	Re-register the accounts and assets of the deceased into the name of the estate, for example, "The estate of..."
❏	❏	❏	Obtain statements showing the value of the deceased's investments as of the date of death.
❏	❏	❏	Obtain statements showing the value of the deceased's RRSPs/RRIFs as of the date of death.
❏	❏	❏	Cancel any pre-authorized savings programs (PACs) or systematic withdrawal programs (SWIP), as well as any pending securities trades.

Started	*Completed*	*Not Applicable*	
❏	❏	❏	Review the investment strategy, and adjust if necessary.
❏	❏	❏	Arrange for the storage of assets requiring it, and advise insurers of any physical assets of the deceased. Arrange for any insurance coverage required.
❏	❏	❏	Review all real estate documents including, deeds, mortgages and leases.
❏	❏	❏	Arrange for valuations of any assets of the estate, such as personal property, real estate, cars, etc.
❏	❏	❏	Cancel the deceased's driver's licence, newspaper, and magazine subscriptions, telephone, cable TV, internet subscription, as well as memberships in any clubs.
❏	❏	❏	Arrange with the post office for mail to be redirected, if necessary, and notify all interested parties of the change of address.
❏	❏	❏	Obtain deeds for real estate, and arrange to sell the real estate if necessary.
❏	❏	❏	Obtain share certificates for bonds, stocks, or GICs not held at a financial institution.
❏	❏	❏	Close the safety deposit box.
❏	❏	❏	Transfer or cancel any insurance policies on the house, car, boat, etc., when appropriate.
❏	❏	❏	Sell any estate assets that must be sold, and those which the personal representative chooses to sell (provided this power is given to the executor in the will).

Settle the Bills of the Estate

Started	*Completed*	*Not Applicable*	
❏	❏	❏	Identify all the liabilities of the deceased.
❏	❏	❏	Determine the outstanding balances of all personal debts.
❏	❏	❏	Arrange for publication of the notice of "Advertisement for Creditors and Others" in a local paper to locate parties who may have a claim against some or all of the estate and would be paid prior to a distribution to any of the beneficiaries.
❏	❏	❏	Cancel all credit cards.
❏	❏	❏	Settle all just claims and debts of the deceased, including credit cards, consumer debts, and mortgages.

Started	*Completed*	*Not Applicable*	
❏	❏	❏	Settle the bills of the estate: creditors, funeral expenses, and other expenses.
❏	❏	❏	Determine if there are sufficient assets in the estate to pay all liabilities and income tax, before making any interim distribution to the beneficiaries, so you do not take on any personal liability for the tax bill.

File the Tax Returns

❏	❏	❏	Prepare and file the tax returns for any years prior to the date of death that have not yet been filed.
❏	❏	❏	Identify opportunities, and make the appropriate elections to reduce the tax bill of the deceased, including using the spousal rollover, applying capital losses, and contributing to a spousal RRSP.
❏	❏	❏	Prepare and file the final tax return for the deceased, as well as any optional returns.
❏	❏	❏	File any tax returns required for assets held outside of Canada, including those required by the IRS.
❏	❏	❏	File estate tax returns (T3) for each year the estate exists, if necessary.
❏	❏	❏	Pay all income taxes due, or obtain an income tax refund, if applicable.
❏	❏	❏	Obtain the tax clearance certificate from Canada Customs and Revenue Agency.

Distribute the Assets of the Estate

❏	❏	❏	Distribute the assets, real estate, and personal property of the estate to the beneficiaries according to the instructions in the will.
❏	❏	❏	Assess any immediate need for cash that the surviving spouse may have.
❏	❏	❏	For accounts registered jointly with rights of survivor, request the account be transferred to the surviving tenant.
❏	❏	❏	Arrange to have the RRSP/RRIF transferred or rolled over to named beneficiaries.
❏	❏	❏	After the tax clearance certificate is obtained, transfer title, and distribute any remaining assets or property in the estate.
❏	❏	❏	Discuss any "in kind" distributions with the beneficiaries.
❏	❏	❏	Complete the paperwork necessary to transfer stocks and other securities.

Started	*Completed*	*Not Applicable*	
❑	❑	❑	Establish any testamentary trusts, according to the instructions in the will.
❑	❑	❑	Obtain receipts and/or release forms from all beneficiaries.

Other

❑	❑	❑	Prepare an accounting of the estate.
❑	❑	❑	Calculate the fees payable to the executor.
❑	❑	❑	Obtain reimbursement for all necessary and reasonable expenses incurred in the administration of the estate (with receipts).
❑	❑	❑	Pay legal fees and all other outstanding fees relating to the administration of the estate.
❑	❑	❑	Pass accounts before a provincial court judge, if necessary.
❑	❑	❑	Close the estate bank account.

Appendix B

LIST OF DUTIES FOR A POWER OF ATTORNEY FOR FINANCIAL DECISIONS

The power of attorney for financial decisions is not a simple document. The document may be very specific as to your duties and responsibilities, including any restrictions placed on your powers. On the other hand, it may be very broad and open-ended. In fact, many power of attorney documents give the attorney the authority to make any and all financial decisions on behalf of the person who prepared the document (except those related to estate planning, such as writing a will).

If you are called upon to be the power of attorney or personal representative for financial decisions, the following checklist outlines some of your duties. However, the responsibilities vary across the country. Unlike the duties of the executor, who is required to act upon the death of the deceased and wrap up the estate, the duties of the power of attorney for financial decisions might last for a short period of time or for many years, ending when the individual regains the capacity to make his or her own decisions, or passes away.

The following partial list of duties and responsibilities is for educational purposes only and is not to be considered as tax, financial, or legal advice.

General

1. Act in the best interests of the individual who appointed you, according to your best judgment.

2. Obtain an original copy of the Power of Attorney (POA) document.

3. Keep the individual's assets, accounts, and bills separate from your own.

4. Obtain an assessment of the individual's mental capacity, if required.

5. Review the instructions in the POA and any restrictions on the attorney's powers.

6. Review all personal papers to help identify and locate his or her assets and debts.

7. Notify all financial institutions that you are acting as the individual's representative. Provide them with the appropriate documentation.

Collect All Income

8. Identify potential sources of income and benefits.

9. Obtain all unpaid wages and other benefits from the individual's current and former employers.

10. Apply for any insurance benefits such as long-term care coverage, critical illness, disability, or living benefits, if applicable.

11. Apply for any government benefits the individual is entitled to receive, such as CPP/QPP, disability benefits, CPP/QPP retirement benefits, and Old Age Security benefits.

12. Apply to the social security office in the U.S. for any benefit entitlement.

13. If the individual was previously in the military, contact the appropriate veteran's office to receive any applicable benefits.

Pay All Bills

14. Review the individual's driver's license, newspaper and magazine subscriptions, telephone, cable TV, and internet subscription, as well as memberships in any clubs. Cancel, if appropriate.

15. Identify all the liabilities of the individual, including the outstanding balances of all personal debts, and make the required payments.

16. Pay all expenditures that are reasonably necessary for the individual's support and care, including food, clothing, accommodation, utilities, dental and medical care and other personal needs, according to the individual's financial resources.

17. Pay expenditures that are reasonably necessary for the support, education, and care of the individual's dependents.

18. Pay expenditures necessary to satisfy any legal obligations the individual has.

19. Adjust the individual cash flow for changes in the individual's needs, such as moving into a nursing home, death of a spouse, etc.

20. Work with the power of attorney for personal and health care to determine how much and when income is required.

Manage Assets

21. Use a prudent standard of care for managing the individual's assets. Adjust the investment strategy, if necessary.

22. Review, and, if necessary, cancel any pre-authorized savings programs (PACs) or systematic withdrawal programs (SWIPs), as well as any pending securities trades.

23. Locate all of the individual's bank accounts and notify the bank that they will be dealing with you.

24. Safeguard the assets, arrange for storage if required, and ensure there is adequate insurance coverage.

25. Review all real estate documents including deeds, mortgages, and leases.

26. Buy, sell, or mortgage real estate if necessary.

27. If the matrimonial home must be sold, and the power of attorney document does not provide the power to sell it under family law, apply to the courts.

28. Buy, sell, or gift personal property.

29. Buy or sell stocks or bonds, or execute any other security transaction.

30. Borrow money on behalf of the individual.

31. Review the contents of the individual's safety deposit box.

32. Make contributions to or withdrawals from registered plans.

33. Make retirement elections for employee pension plans.

34. Manage any sums of money received, such as an inheritance, divorce, or injury settlement.

Tax and Legal

35. File the individual's tax return on an annual basis.

36. File any tax returns required for assets held outside of Canada, including those required by the IRS.

37. Pay all income taxes due, or obtain an income tax refund, if applicable.

38. File for an income tax re-assessment, if necessary.

39. Act as the individual's personal representative with the Canada Customs and Revenue Agency.

40. Act on the individual's behalf regarding claims and lawsuits.

41. Mediate or arbitrate disputes on the individual's behalf.

42. Represent the individual's interest in any estate or trust claims.

43. Sign legal documents on behalf of the individual.

44. Pay legal fees and all other fees for the individual.

Other

45. If more than one person has been appointed as the power of attorney, work together to make decisions on behalf of the individual who prepared the power of attorney document.

46. Obtain legal, tax, or financial advice.

47. Receive reimbursement for all reasonable out-of-pocket expenses related to performing these duties.

48. Reimburse the power of attorney for personal and health care for all reasonable out-of-pocket expenses related to performing those duties.

49. Calculate your compensation, if any.

50. Maintain full and accurate records of all activities, receipts, and disbursements made on behalf of the individual.

51. If someone has been appointed to monitor or oversee the decisions you make, provide them with an accounting of all your activities and financial decisions, as required.

52. Review the will so you better understand the individual's wishes.

53. On death, transfer the accounts to the estate executor and trustee.

Your duties end on the death of the individual. The power of attorney document is powerless after death.

Appendix C

LIST OF DUTIES FOR A POWER OF ATTORNEY FOR PERSONAL AND HEALTH CARE DECISIONS

The power of attorney for personal and health care may be very specific as to your duties and responsibilities, including any restrictions placed on your powers. On the other hand, it may be very broad and leave many of the decisions to your discretion, provided you act in the individual's best interest. If the individual has not left instructions for you to follow, or has not discussed with you his or her wishes, you must make decisions based on what you believe is in the individual's best interest.

Generally, you will only be called upon when, and if, the individual becomes incapable of making his or her own decisions, or when it is reasonable to believe he or she is no longer capable of making a required decision.

If you are called upon to be the power of attorney or personal representative for personal and health care, the following checklist outlines some of your duties and responsibilities. If you are not also named as the power of attorney for financial decisions, you will need to consult with those who are, particularly for those that depend on the individual's financial means.

The following partial list of duties and responsibilities of the power of attorney for personal and health care is for educational purposes only and is not to be considered as tax, financial, or legal advice.

General

1. Act in the best interests of the individual who appointed you, according to your best judgment.

2. Obtain an original copy of the power of attorney document for personal and health care.

3. Review the instructions in the power of attorney document and any restrictions on the attorney's powers or special requests.

4. Obtain an assessment of the individual's mental capacity, if required.

5. Notify the individual's doctor, dentist, and other health-care providers that you are the power of attorney for personal and health care matters.

6. Identify all expenditures that are reasonably necessary for the individual's support and care, including food, clothing, accommodation, utilities, dental and medical care, and other personal needs.

7. Work with the power of attorney for financial decisions to determine how much income is available.

8. If more than one person has been appointed as the power of attorney, work together to make decisions on behalf of the individual who prepared the power of attorney document.

9. Apply for a disability tax credit certificate, if applicable.

Decisions Related to Personal Care

10. Decide where the person will live, including whether or not he or she needs to move into an assisted-living or long-term care facility.

11. Make day-to-day decisions regarding what the individual will wear and who may visit.

12. Consider the individual's dietary restrictions when planning his or her menus.

Decisions Related to Medical Care

13. Arrange regular medical and dental check-ups.

14. Consent to appropriate medical tests, including exploratory surgery, as well as required major surgery on behalf of the individual.

15. Release medical records and history when it is required.

16. Consent to participate in medical research studies or experimental treatments, if appropriate.

17. Withhold medical treatment you believe the individual would not want.

18. If it would have been the individual's wish, do not allow his or her life to be prolonged, if there is no reasonable expectation of recovery, such as during the final stages of a terminal illness.

19. Arrange for palliative care.

20. Take legal action on the individual's behalf if necessary, related to the powers that have been granted.

Other

21. Contact the power of attorney for financial decisions for reimbursement for all reasonable out-of-pocket expenses related to performing your duties.

22. Calculate your compensation, if any.

23. Maintain full and accurate records of all activities made on behalf of the individual.

24. If someone has been appointed to monitor or oversee the decisions you make, provide them with an accounting of all your activities, as required.

Your duties end on the death of the individual.

Glossary

adjusted cost base   Used in calculating capital gains tax. The amount paid for an asset or property, plus commissions and other expenses.

administrator   Person appointed by the provincial court to carry out the duties of the executor when a person dies intestate (without a will), or with a will that does not name an executor.

advanced health care directive   A document, or clauses in your power of attorney for personal and health care document, that indicates your wishes regarding the refusal of, or consent to, medical treatment and who should decide for you if you are unable to. It often lists a number of specific scenarios, and for each scenario, the specific medical treatments you wish to be used, or wish not be used.

affidavit of execution   A document signed by your witness certifying that the signing and witnessing of your will followed proper procedures.

alter ego trust   A living trust to which you can transfer your personal assets if you are age 65 or older to minimize probate fees and taxes.

attribution rule   From CCRA's perspective, the person who is responsible for paying the tax on income earned, even after certain assets are given away.

beneficiary   A person or charity named in the will, life insurance policy, RRSP/RRIF, segregated funds, pension plan, or trust to receive benefits.

bequest   A gift in your will.

buy-sell agreement   Agreement between business owners or partners dealing with buying out their portion of the business in the event of death, disability, or retirement.

capital gain   A profit on an asset or property.

Canada Customs and Revenue Agency   Formerly called Revenue Canada.

CCRA   Canada Customs and Revenue Agency, formerly called Revenue Canada

charitable remainder trust   A gift made to a registered charity using a living trust where the donor continues to receive income/benefits from the assets donated. When the donor dies, any remaining assets in the trust transfer to the charity.

codicil   A legal change to a will.

committee   The legal guardian of an adult with developmental or mental disabilities. Used in B.C., Manitoba, New Brunswick, and PEI.

curator   The term used in Quebec for "legal guardian."

deemed disposition   When CCRA considers that assets and property are sold at fair market value even if no actual sale took place. This happens on death and when people emigrate from Canada.

dependents   Family members who are dependent on you for financial support.

devise   A gift made in the will.

donor   A person making a gift, such as to charity, or through an organ donation.

escheat   The process, if you die without a will and have no living relatives, whereby the provincial government becomes the beneficiary of last resort.

executor   Person or trust company named in the will to follow out the instructions in the will when the person who made the will dies. Female is called an executrix. Also liquidator, estate trustee, or personal representative.

family trust   A trust set up for family members, such as for underage children who cannot hold assets directly or for family members who cannot handle money or who have special needs. Also see spousal trust.

fiduciary   Person acting on behalf of another who has an obligation to act in good faith and fair dealing, such as an executor, trustee, or financial advisor.

guardian   The person responsible for the care of a child under the age of majority or for someone who is incompetent. A legal guardian is appointed through the courts.

heir   Person receiving an inheritance through a will. Also called a beneficiary.

holograph will   A will written completely in a person's own handwriting and signed at the end by the person writing the will. No witnesses are required.

in kind   Something given as a good, service, or commodity, such as a stock or car, rather than cash.

inter vivos trust   A living, or inter vivos trust, where assets are transferred into the trust while the settlor is alive and generally taxed at the top tax rate

intestate   Dying without a will.

IPP   Individual pension plan, as opposed to a group pension plan

irrevocable   That which cannot be changed or cancelled.

joint tenancy   Assets or property that is owned jointly with others. May be joint tenants, with rights of survivorship, or joint tenants in common.

letters probate   Paperwork issued by the provincial court when the will and the paperwork submitted by your executor are in good order. In Ontario, letters probate are referred to as "the certificate of appointment of estate trustee with a will," i.e., the certificate of appointment of your executor under the will.

life insurance policy   One aspect of estate planning. A contractual agreement with a life insurance company to pay your beneficiaries a tax-free death benefit in exchange for premiums you pay during your lifetime.

liquidator   Executor in Quebec.

living trust   Inter vivos trusts, or living trusts, are established primarily for family, tax, or estate planning reasons and are set up during the settlor's lifetime. They are taxed at the top tax rate.

living will   An advanced health care directive that indicates your wishes regarding the types or degree of health care or medical intervention you would like to receive or refuse when you are unable to speak for yourself. A living will may be part of your power of attorney for personal and health care. It is misnamed because it is not a will and it deals with your dying, not your living.

mandate   In Quebec, a power of attorney document.

medical directive   A document, or clauses in your personal care document, that allows a person to indicate the types of medical treatments they would like, or not like, applied for their situation.

minor   Someone who has not yet reached the age of majority.

palliative care   Medical care provided for the terminally ill to make them comfortable by relieving symptoms.

per stirpes   Where a beneficiary (such as a child) predeceases you, the gift that would have been theirs passes on to the next generation (your grandchildren, their children).

power of attorney for property   A document in which you appoint a person to make financial decisions on your behalf. The authority given is valid only while you are alive—it stops on death. The person(s) named may be the same person as your executor—but they get their authority from completely separate documents. Referred to by different names in different provinces.

probate   The process in which the provincial court reviews your will after death, declares it valid, and collects a probate fee or tax. If everything is in order, probate gives your executor the authority to settle your estate, commonly referred to as "letters probate."

probate fee   A fee (in some provinces called a tax) charged on the value of the assets that flow through the will probated by the courts.

public trustee   The public trustee (also called the official guardian or children's lawyer) in your province, who among other things, makes decisions on behalf of minor children who do not have a parent or legal guardian, or on behalf of individuals who cannot make decisions for themselves, unless they have appointed a substitute decision maker.

residue   The portion of the estate remaining after all taxes, bills, bequests, fees, and expenses have been paid.

segregated funds   The insurance industry's answer to mutual funds.

spendthrift trust   A trust for a spendthrift, someone who is not a good money manager, who "spends the results of someone else's thriftiness."

spousal trust   A testamentary trust set up under a will to hold property and assets for the exclusive benefit of a surviving spouse. It may be established using some or all of the inheritance.

tax clearance certificate   A certificate from CCRA (or the Minister of Revenue in Quebec) to the executor that no more income tax is owed by the deceased.

testamentary trust   A trust set up in your last will and testament. No assets or property are in the trust until after the estate is settled.

testator   A person who prepares a "last will and testament."

trust   A formal arrangement where the legal owner (settlor) transfers assets or property into a legal entity to be managed on behalf of the beneficiaries.

trustee   A person or institution appointed in a trust agreement to manage the assets for the beneficiaries.

U.S. situs   Located in the United States.

will   An estate planning document that indicates the instructions of the deceased for distributing assets and property to his or her chosen beneficiaries and the name of the executor

SUGGESTIONS AND SEMINARS

Founded by Sandra Foster, Headspring Consulting Inc.'s mandate is to provide quality, independent advice, education and expertise to the financial services industry and Canadians.

Services Include:

- Consumer education through books and presentations
- Professional development programs
- Strategic advice

For More Information, Visit:

www.headspringconsulting.com

www.whosmindingyourmoney.com

If you have any comments or are interested in a presentation or workshop for your group or association, please contact us through one of the methods below:

By email   fosters@headspringconsulting.com

By fax   416 494 9530

Through the publisher   John Wiley & Sons Canada, Ltd.
22 Worcester Road
Etobicoke, Ontario M9W 1L1

Available Summer 2002

ORDER FORM

To order copies of the interactive *Estate Planning Worksheets* on CD-ROM, for personal use please complete the following information.
For more information, email: info@headspringconsulting.com
or fax inquiry to (416) 494-9530.

ESTATE PLANNING WORKSHEETS CD-ROM _____ copies at $29.95 ea. = _____

Shipping & Handling* _____

(*$6.00 for each CD-ROM,

$3.00 for each additional CD-ROM)

Taxes Included

AMOUNT ENCLOSED _____

PLEASE PRINT

❑ Mr.   ❑ Mrs.   ❑ Miss   ❑ Ms.

_____   _____
Last Name   First Name

_____   _____
Address   Apt.#

_____   _____
City   Province   Postal Code

(_____) _____   _____
Phone   E-mail

❑ Enclosed is a cheque or money order for $_____ payable to Headspring Consulting Inc.

MAIL THIS COUPON TO:
Estate Planning Worksheets
c/o Headspring Consulting Inc.
1370 Don Mill Road, Suite 300, Toronto, ON M3B 3N7

Licences are available for corporations to use the *Estate Planning Worksheets* with their clients.
For more information, email info@headspringconsulting.com.

NOTES

NOTES

NOTES

NOTES

NOTES

NOTES

NOTES

NOTES